COACH

"The Mediator Of Dreams And Destroyer Of Generations"

BASED ON A TRUE STORY

Jerry "Bobo" Mason

Dwight,

Thanks for the support bro. I've appreciated getting to know you better over the years. I truly love you and your family bro. I hope you enjoy the book F.

Jerry
"Bobo"
Mason

Printed in the United States Of America

ISBN - 13: 978-0-578-71908-5

Contact Informaiton:

Jerry "Bobo" Mason
AuthorJerryMason@gmail.com

Cover design by: Carlos V. Kaigler
C'Vaughn'K Graphic Design / The Poet B.GKL

Bibliography: Dr. Patricia Demps
DPD
PUBLISHING

JERRY"BOBO"MASON

COACH

"The Mediator of Dreams And Destroyer of Generations"

Written By:
Jerry "Bobo" Mason

AN UNDERDSTANDING OF THE POWERFUL OR DEVASTING IMPACT COACHES HAVE DURING A SPORTS JOURNEY AND THE EFFECTS BECAUSE OF, THAT WILL LAST A LIFETIME.

DEDICATION

God for life, love and the ability to think, feel, see, believe and persevere through all the obstacles the devil put in front of me.

My beautiful Momma, Velma, who's shining down on me from heaven and who raised me beautifully to be the man I am today. I LOVE AND MISS YOU MOMMA.

My Daddy, Jerry, who instilled discipline, toughness, wisdom and fight into my brothers, sister and myself.

My brothers, Chris and Cedric, and my sister, Monique, for love, companion-ship, friendship, competition and MASON pride.

My sons, Jeremy and Jordan for allowing me to be your Dad. For giving me the chance to make amends so that we can be close and be a family. For being good to and for other people.

All my teammates I ever played with from youth sports all the way through college. To all the players I've been blessed to teach, coach and mentor during my coaching journey. To all the coaches that I have coached with that have helped me perfect my craft as a coach.

All of my coaches who helped mold me from a kid to the man I am today; and inspired me to become a published author.

INTRODUCTION:

THINGS

SOME THINGS MEAN MORE TO US, THAN OTHERS EVER WILL,

BECAUSE NO ONE SHOULD TELL US WHAT WE WANT OR HOW WE NEED TO FEEL.

SOME THINGS WILL NEVER BE, THE WAY WE THINK THEY SHOULD,

BECAUSE IF THEY WERE, THERE WOULD BE NO CHALLENGE AND LIFE WOULD BE TOO GOOD.

SOME THINGS WILL NEVER CHANGE, THEY WILL KEEP CHINGLING LIKE SOUNDS FROM CHIMES,

SO THEREFORE, I TRY TO EXPRESS TO YOU, MY UP AND DOWN TIMES.

SOME THINGS WILL STING A LITTLE AND SOME WILL CUT LIKE A KNIFE,

AND FROM THAT I TRY TO PATCH THE PIECES AND WRITE FOR YOU, MY LIFE.

JERRY "BOBO" MASON

PROLOGUE

... *"you've got to give the man a chance stud. The season hasnt even started yet. I think everything is going to be better than you think".*

I said to him angrily,

" dad, this isn't something I'm thinking, this is what I know and what I feel".

But my dad was persistent wiht his belief and told me to stick it out and see how it goes. Therefore, I did.

It was a crushing reality to the beginning of my new journey.

Coach Roberts Would say to me,

"Bo, I feel very lucky to be your coach, you are great and only going to get better from there".

Coach Carlesimo said to me,

"Jerry you are going to be great here at Seton Hall. You are going to do things these people have never seen. With you here Jerry, we can win a national championship".

Coach Myers said to me,

"YOU'RE GOING TO HAVE A HARD TIME PLAY- ING HERE BECAUSE YOU CAN'T PLAY DEFENSE".

I could have been one of the best players he ever had if he would have let me do it my way. However, my way was more extraordinary than he had ever had. Therefore, in order to contain my greatness, he tried to embed in me I couldn't play defense. I'm a winner. When He'd say that, I'd think, "if cant play defense, I just didn't walk on to Texas Tech campus and now I can't play. If I can't play now, I couldn't play defense in Lamesa. So why would you come recruit me and interfere with my plans to attend another university if you didn't like my defense?" "Why come get me just to degrade me?" "Why you come to me and want me to be a lesser version of who I was when you got me? Why come get me to belittle me?"

Coach Myers didn't want stars, he wanted puppets. The problem was I wasn't a puppet for no one.

COACH

I remember the first coach I ever had. Mr. David Lee Smith. We called him "coach". He was not a certified coach by means of the teaching system. Most of the coaches who coach and teach Pee Wee League baseball are not. I was a first-grader, but boy was he qualified to me. Being a "Certified" Coach means a coach passed all of the mandated requirements and tests to be valid to teach and coach within the teaching system. This really doesn't apply much to youth league sports; being certified that is. But a qualified coach passes all the blessings of God to be able to help each kid along their journey to success. I will elaborate more on certified and qualified throughout this journey.

Coach Smith gave us an opportunity by picking us on the team. Just a simple opportunity with kids can go a long way. He provided us with things that would impact my life forever. With everything he provided for us, he explained why they were important and how it would impact our present and future. Coach Smith was a qualified coach and teacher. Before we started actual baseball, he explained to us the importance of our senses. He first told us our senses (sound, sight, touch, smell, and taste) were tremendous blessings from God. But also, that those same senses were crucial to being good in sports. Coach Smith taught the senses of touch and sound with bats.

He provided our team with two bats. He provided us with a wooden bat and an aluminum bat with a marble inside. Let me explain how these two bats he provided for us changed my senses forever.

This is when the addiction to sports first started for me. Although we were young, we could play some baseball. Coach Smith, top left, was the catalyst for my beginning and understanding of greatness.

[I am 3rd from the right and Chris 2nd from the left.]

BASEBALL BATS

Baseball is the first love of a lot of young kids because it's the first youth sport you can play. At least when I was a kid it was. Baseball was the drug. Baseball was the drug that provided me addiction. It was that, that would awaken, shape, and mold the rest of my life. It was a good addiction. My Pee Wee team was named Jones McCall Pharmacy. My brother Chris and I along with a lot of my neighborhood friends were all on this team. Coach Smith was a parent coach. He had three sons on the team (David, Tommy, and Prentice). A lot of the children playing beginner or youth sports are taught by one or both of their parents.

As I stated earlier, Coach Smith provided the team with two bats. The sounds of two bats created dialogue for us. The noise those two bats made upon contact heightened our sense of sound and the understanding of the impact of sound. It was a life-changing experience to learn. These are things that Coach Smith taught us as very young children. When impact was made with the wooden bat, it made a "crack" sound. It sounded like an explosion of fireworks. When impact was made with the aluminum bat, it made a "ping" sound. Coach Smith taught us that by the impact of the sound of each bat when contact is made with the ball, what kind of hit it may be. We could tell if it was a home run, pop up, bunt, hard-hit ball, or a weak hit ball. By learning this, it helped us no matter what position we played on defense. It helped us judge the power and distance of the hit ball. Not only did the bats heighten our sense of sound, but they gave us our individual opinion and a voice for what we heard.

Sometimes we would walk from one field to another to watch

the older kids play. In each park, while walking, we could tell what kind of hit it was by the sound of the contact. We could tell if it was a wooden or aluminum

Sometimes we would be walking from one field to another to watch the older kids. In each park while walking, we could tell what kind of hit it was by the sounds of the contact. We could tell if it was a wooden or aluminum bat without seeing it. Just sounds. The bats gave us the gift of pride, sharing, possession, awareness and excitement. They were our bats. Being a good coach is more than just providing a kid with words and wisdom. Everything about the journey matters. The first team or uniform most kids experience will be the experience that they will always remember. They will judge their progress based on who they used to be and how they wore that hat or even how that uniform fit. It is the responsibility of the parents and coaches of young kids to make sure that youth sports are a fun experience. Allow them to fail without judgment and teach them to grow within that failure. Make the experience so enjoyable that the kids want to play sports for the rest of their lives.

THE UNIFORM

Coach Smith also provided us with the uniform. Baseball was my first uniform. The Jones McCall Pharmacy uniform. The jersey was blue with white letters along with the hat and the pants were white. We even had blue leggings. It was awesome. Individually each piece of the uniform had its own life and purpose. Its own purpose in shaping of our individual identities, team accomplishments and a separation from the "we". The hat was ours but the way we bent, molded, shaped and wore it gave us our own identity. It defined who and what we were trying to be. With all the folds and bends of the hat, we put our own individual touches and the hat made us "me".

This is what so many coachers fear. Their kids having their own identity within the "we". Even though the uniform made us a team, Coach Smith allowed us as kids to form our own image and swag. It's so important for kids of all levels to have a chance to put their own personality on their journey. The way we molded and wore our hats said, "this is me. This is who I am". The uniform was our "us". We are Jones McCall Pharmacy. The colors made us one. The jersey made us relevant and gave us a constant belonging. The jersey made us family. The jersey made us team. The jersey made us rivals. The jersey made us competitors. The jersey gave us a brotherhood, protection and a desire to protect. The jersey made us love winning and despise losing. The jersey gave us our heart.

Parents do not take youth sports for granted. They are the foundation for kids for more than just sports. By Coach Smith picking us, it made us feel wanted. Also, parents make sure if your kids do play youth sports that the coach is qualified. Make sure that he's not only a caretaker but a teacher as well.

Coach Smith took care of us. He taught us more than base-ball. He taught us how the equipment used in baseball applied to life. He was our foundation for fun, discipline, learning, sacrifice, team, love and winning. Make sure your kids' coach or coaches are providing the same. Coach Smith was not only a great man but a great mentor. We were able to learn these life changing things as kids. Wherever we would go from that point, he provided us a base. He provided us a reference point we could use to find our way. Something we could trust. He provided us a chance to learn and know ourselves. A chance to trust others while learning ourselves. Make sure when your kid calls a person "coach", that person deserves it. It should not be an order to be called "coach", but a blessing.

We loved everything about baseball. More than anything, we loved each other and had fun sitting and watching more baseball. We also took pride in our swag. I am left on the front row and Chris on the left the row behind me.

MY YOUNG JOURNEY

Even though I loved and still played baseball, Lamesa was a basketball town. Basketball was tradition. That tradition and history put the pressure on us as kids and the coaches we had to make sure tradition was maintained. We couldn't start playing Little Dribblers basketball until 3rd grade. We started baseball in the 1st grade. But because of baseball, we already knew what team meant. We already knew the value and honor of the uniform. We already knew how to compete. We already knew how to win and be champions. I forgot to state earlier that my Jones McCall Pharmacy team never lost a game. We were winners and champions already and it was addicting. Little Dribblers continued building and shaping us as Coach Smith did.

Because Lamesa was a small town, all the parents and volunteer coaches shared the same vision when it came to sports. Some parents were coaches. Coach Smith was a parent coach. My dad Jerry was one of my Little Dribbler coaches. He too as a kid played all sports. He was All State in basketball in high school and was also a member of the 1967 state champion basketball team. We had coaches that understood what we had learned. Not all of them were or had been All State in a sport. But they understood what it took to be winners. Because of that, they taught us and gave us an opportunity to be winners. I am not saying they were easy on us. I'm not saying because some were parents that they gave us a pass. As a matter of fact, it was the total opposite. They yelled at us. They got mad at us. They pushed us.

My dad and his swag. Like Pee Wee baseball, I loved winning trophies in Little Dribblers basketball. Also, like baseball, I had great coaches in youth basketball as well.

They made us say "yes sir" and "no sir". They expected us to compete and win. They taught us how to be good winners and better losers. They made us cry without showing empathy. We hated them at times. But the greatest thing they did was never do anything without explaining why it hampered or benefited us. They never yelled or pushed for their benefit. They did it for our benefit and explained how and why. That's what qualified coaches do. They don't sugar coat. They don't pretend. They don't interject their dreams or failed dreams into the kids' journey. They push hard. They yell at times. They expect and enforce discipline, respect and courtesy. They love hard and they feel deep. They learn the kids and what the kids dream to be. From that, they make sure they push and teach and do whatever necessary to help EACH kid continue to improve and on the path to THEIR dream.

YOUTH COACHES

The good thing about Lamesa is that it was a small town. We all played all the sports and learned and grew together. No matter what race or size, our coaches expected the same from us all. It is imperative parents to make sure youth coaches know their role. They're need to know their role is to be knowledge-able of their sport they are coaching. They should be able to translate that knowledge in a positive manner. A manner that will benefit each kid. They need to understand the age group they are coaching and base expectations on that level. Some kids will develop physically faster than others. It's the coaches' responsibility to enhance all and not play favoritism. Youth coaches need to teach the fundamentals of the sport they are coaching correctly. They need to be positive, patient and reinforcing while teaching the fundamentals.

The youth coaches I had when I played sports pounded and bored us with fundamentals. In doing so, they provided me with a base that allowed me to be mentally and physically skilled and prepared. It also allowed a base for me to assess myself. Meaning, if something was going wrong while I was playing, it was probably something with my fundamentals and I could fix it myself. Youth coaches are probably the most in-strumental figures in the lives of young kids who play sports. They can help propel the athletes towards their dream or be instrumental in ruining their joy and making them hate sports. Parents who coach their kids need to make sure they aren't so overbearing that they cause their own kid to despise playing sports. Parents need to make sure the coaches are passion-ate about their kids physical and mental growth. I had great coaches throughout my youth and elementary years. Every-thing I became is because I was taught well while playing

youth sports.

TRANSITION

In this transition I will be traveling from my youth sports to my secondary sports journey. I consider youth and elementary sports 1st-6th grades and secondary from 7th-12th grades. Any sports played after 12th grade I consider a blessing. Also, throughout this journey I will deviate from past into present time. I will do so to show how opportunities for kids have grown. But I will also show that no matter how many opportunities exist, explain why coaches are still the most important figures in the advancement and demise of athletes. I will show how some of my coaches assisted in helping some of my dreams come true while one ruined me and generations to come. My hope with telling my journey is to help kids and families understand the importance of finding the right school with the right coach. Things they need to know and ask before committing to any school or coach at any level including private schools and AAU sports.

A topic I want to elaborate on before embarking on my secondary journey is Certified vs. Qualified. Coach Smith and my other youth sports coaches provided me with every opportunity to be great. They provided opportunities for me to have, explore, desire and grow. They were qualified men and qualified coaches.

CERTIFIED VS. QUALIFIED

Once a kid is provided an opportunity to experience, feel, touch, attain and embrace success, it becomes addictive. That kid becomes a dreamer. The dream itself is an addiction. To be able to understand the addiction, this is what a qualified coach does. To be knowledgeable enough to understand and assist that kid in his or her dream. To allow that kid every opportunity possible to achieve and live out that dream to the fullest of God's blessing. Certified fills the void for the non-certified. Qualified fills the void for the blessing. Qualified fills the cracks in the holes of the dreams and lets God's destiny do the rest. Certified coaches usually become more in effect when an athlete enters Jr. High. There are certified teachers and P.E. teachers in elementary schools, but most certified coaches begin in Jr. High. Certified means that the coach graduated from an accredited college and passed the required exams to be certified to teach and coach. Most Jr. High coaches teach a core subject along with coaching two or three sports.

Being a teacher and coach for 26 years, I've taught elementary, Jr. High and high school kids. Each level requires a different understanding of the kids' maturity process as they start to build the foundation of who they want to be. In Jr. High, kids are really trying to find themselves. Unfortunately, so are beginning, just getting certified coaches. They too are just starting out and trying to build their own foundation. They aren't yet qualified to deal with the difficulties many Jr. High kids go through, especially young athletes. This is when a lot of young athletes fail to get the necessary teaching and development they need. A lot of them fall behind, get discouraged and quit playing sports for good. Just because the coach or coaches were not qualified enough to foster the athletic needs and desires of the kids. Just because a coach is certified, doesn't mean he or she is qualified. All certified doctors aren't qualified doctors. All certified referees aren't great referees. It's the same in all professions. If you as a parent aren't satisfied with a restaurant, doctor, dentist, toothpaste or lawyer, you find another. So, if you have a kid or kids that love a sport or sports and has the desire to play college or professional sports, find the right school and coach to assist in the journey. It's not good as parents to tell your kid or kids they can't or will not be a college or professional athlete. Let them dream. Your job as parents is to put them in the proper places with the right people who can help facilitate their dreams.

MY JR. HIGH JOURNEY

Jr. High for me was probably the worst two years of my life as a kid. It wasn't because the coaches I had even though the coaching was different than I had in youth sports. It was different because the expectations were more about the schools' reputation and success as opposed to the athletes. The coaches dictated where they thought you should go or play instead of you playing where you wanted to play. In youth sports there were many teams where everybody had a chance to be primary. In Jr. High there were two, A team and B team. Coach Wedding was our Jr. High football coach. He was all about the business of the school. I never knew if he was a good coach or not. What I did know is since youth sports All-Stars we didn't lose much if any at all. We didn't lose a game in 7th grade football. However, the issue wasn't winning and losing. The issue came with the A and the B teams. In youth sports we all felt equal. Some of the kids that made All-Stars in youth sports made the B team in football. Some of the kids that didn't make All-Stars in youth sports made the A team.

Coach Weddings decision to who played on the A and B created a lot of different emotions we never had to deal with in youth sports. That A and that B really meant something. That's when I learned how separation began. That's when I learned how pretending began. Those on the A team had to make our childhood friends on the B team feel that they were the same team. Those on the B team had to pretend they weren't heartbroken and confused. That's when I learned about politics. That's when I learned some players on the A team who I know were not better football players than some on the B team parents had money and clout in the district and town. That's when I learned that even though they were the first two letters of the alphabet, A and B, they were more powerful than the rest of the letters combined.

Coach Fitch was our Jr. High basketball coach. We gave him
instant credibility because he played college basketball with
Maurice Cheeks at West Texas A&M. Maurice Cheeks played in
the NBA with the 76ers. We instantly thought Coach Fitch was
qualified because of that. He did teach us some things a little
more advanced than we had learned in Little Dribblers. But because Lamesa was a basketball tradition town, we were already
pretty good from playing basketball almost every day. However, this is when the worst two years of my life to that point
began.

On the day of my first Jr. High basketball game, I was running
at lunch and felt and heard a snap in my right foot. It was a pain
I would not wish on my worst enemy. It was a pain no human
should ever feel, especially not a young teenager. I could
barely walk. But the fear of me never getting a chance to play
basketball caused me to hide the extent of my injury. I could
not hide the injury because the limp was so visible. However,
to that point, I had never shown anyone my foot. Even though
it was visibly broken. Not even my parents. I played two years
of sports as if I had a sprained ankle. I learned how to manage
the pain and walk and run as if I were getting better. But the
pain and the swelling made it very difficult for me. I only aver-
aged 4 points per game in the 7th grade. What made Coach Fitch
a good coach was that he never made me feel bad about my out-
put even though the expectations were high for me because my
dad was a living basketball legend.

My self- esteem during those two years was as low as I'm sure
self- esteem could get. I sucked. My 8th grade year wasn't much
better. But my coaches never judged or gave up on me. They
gave me chances to work through whatever I said it was and
them not ever knowing what it was. But it was the pain that
made Jr. High so horrible for me. I also learned a lot about my-

self. I learned that if I was willing to go through the pain I experienced to continue playing, that basketball was my world. Because I went through so much pain and agony during this time, the way my journey ended hurts much more. I'm very broken to this day because of the way my journey ended and so is my foot.

SOME DREAMS DIE EARLY

It's sometimes hard to see the impact of coaching in Jr. High. But the coaching is very crucial. Some kids are growing faster than others. Coaches that are not qualified usually show favoritism toward the bigger, faster or more aggressive kids. Those kids are more dominant and can provide the coaches immediate results. The coaches aren't qualified enough to understand that the kid you see in 7th and 8th grade won't be the young man that evolves throughout high school. In Jr. High basketball and volleyball kids are usually judged by their height. If the kid is tall, he's a post or she's a blocker. In football, coaches position kids based on their size, weight and body build. This is usually done even if the kid wants to play another position. This is when Jr. High coaching has its greatest negative impact on kids. It has a negative impact on them mentally. That's why the impact is so hard to visualize. When kids have coaches telling them," you're too little, too short, too slow, too tall or you can't do this or you can't do that", it affects them mentally. It happens a lot in Jr. High coaches telling kids what they think the kid should be instead of helping the kids be who the kids desire to be.

When I got my first Head basketball coaching job at Ennis High School, I immediately went to the Jr. High. I wanted to talk with one of the 8th grade athletes, Timmy Barnes. I asked one of the Jr. High coaches to call him over to me. He was a big kid for Jr. High. More overweight than muscle, but a good size. I told him once he came from 8th to 9th grade, he was going to play varsity basketball for me. I told him this even though he had played on the B team two years at the Jr. High. He was very excited as he walked off. The Jr. High coach then laughed and said to me, "coach that boy can't walk and chew gum at the same time". I responded, "yeah coach that's sad he's been here with you for two years and you haven't taught him how to do neither? Walk or chew gum?"

Along with Timmy, I would start two other Freshmen on the varsity. By the time Timmy, Jordan and Kyle graduated in 2012, they had put Ennis basketball on the map. They helped lead Ennis to a district championship, multiple playoff wins and had offers from college basketball schools.

Timmy Barnes holding champions trophy after beating powerhouse Desoto High School in the championship.

[Kyle Anderson to his right and Jordan Mason to his left.]

So many dreams die early in Jr. High because of coaches like this coach. Instead of helping the kids with what they know they can't do, they make fun of the kids. Therefore, because of embarrassment or low self- esteem, the kids quit sports. This is the difference between certified and qualified coaches. It is very important parents that you don't wait until high school to be concerned about the impact coaches can have on your kids' journey. The real journey may never begin.

Make sure you do your homework about the Jr. High district you move into and the school you send your kid to. When looking for a Jr. High, make sure the school has at least one primary coach in the sport or sports your kids desire to play. A lot of one sport dominated schools hire most of their Jr. High coaches based on that sport. Because football is so popular, a lot of the times most Jr. High coaches will be football primary. But there are also schools where basketball, volleyball and baseball are the primary sport. What I mean by primary, is that one sport may win state championships, district championships or make the playoffs every year while the other sports aren't winning. So that winning sport becomes the primary sport and the primary hire for the Jr. High coaches. There are schools where there is no primary sport based on winning. But, one sport may be promoted or desired to be the primary sport.

No matter what the case is parents, make sure you find out before sending your kid to any school or coach. It is very important you know these things before moving into a district. Because I broke my foot, my Jr. High coaches didn't have much of an opportunity to affect me mentally. Not that they would have. I was mentally ruined because of the trauma and pain and the fear from both that I would not excel. Because of this, as I progress through my next journey, coaching becomes life changing for me.

AN UNDERSTANDING

Throughout the rest of the book I will take you on my final journeys. I will deviate to and from my playing career, coaching career and my life as it is because of each. Parents never underestimate how engulfing sports can be within the soul of your kids. In the process of writing this journey, I will have been coaching for 26 years. Four years at All Saints Episcopal School as an elementary P.E. teacher and Jr. High coach. 17 1/2 years at Ennis High School as P.E. teacher, cross country coach and basketball coach and 5 years at Terrell High school as a P.E. teacher and basketball coach. I want my coaching history known because as I write about my journey, I want you to know I'm writing from true experiences. I also want kids reading my journey to embrace who they are for them to embrace their journey. I want them to be able to understand and pay attention to elements that will assist or derail their journey. For them to know that it is possible to persevere through the ups and downs and positives and negatives of their journey. More importantly, for them to be able to recognize a coach that is good or bad for them and to take advantage of the situation or get away from it.

Throughout my journey through high school, you will not hear my high school basketball coach's name a lot. You won't hear it a lot because he was a great qualified coach. You won't hear it a lot because he gave me the opportunity and let it be my journey. He taught me and let me build on that. He gave me light and allowed me to walk, kick, push or whatever I chose to do through it. He allowed me to be the puppet master of my own puppet show. He allowed me to be me or whomever I wanted to incorporate within me. That's what a great coach does. He provides for you. From there, he enjoys the journey with you, the good and the bad. That's what Wayne Roberts did for me. He gave me a chance to build my own reputation through his opportunity. He gave me a chance to gain fans, sign autographs for kids and achieve awards that I never thought I'd have a chance to achieve when I broke my foot. Wayne Roberts saved my life without even knowing it. So much pain and heartache.

So much fear and doubt. So many lonely miserable nights I had since I had broken my foot in the 7th grade.

Wayne Roberts gave me a chance and as bad as my foot was still hurting, I ran with it. As you read my high school basketball journey, know that all the wins, fun, opportunities and accolades I had and achieved are all because of a great man, mentor and coach, Wayne Roberts.

BIG TIME

I began my high school basketball journey on the freshmen team. High school basketball was much different than Jr. High. It was different because of the pressure of being in high school. My foot was better but still broken. I had learned to manage, adjust and work through the pain. I so desperately wanted to be playing on the varsity team. It was always my dream. To run out of that dressing room in front of a packed crowd wearing that Lamesa Golden Tornado uniform. It was an awesome event. Lamesa basketball game night was like a festival. It seemed like on game nights every store, business and restaurant closed early. Everyone was at the basketball game. It tore me deep in my soul because I wanted to be a part of the show. I wanted to be the show. I wanted to be the reason people left work early. I wanted to be the reason kids played basketball. I wanted to be the reason people envied my mom for being my mom. Lamesa basketball was iconic.

When I got to high school, Lamesa basketball had already won several state championships. The basketball history and tradition in Lamesa was rich. My dad was a member of a state championship team. I had uncles and cousins that were members of state championship teams. They always let us know it. The pressure to maintain tradition loomed, but I wanted more than can be imagined. I would always go by Coach Roberts' office during my freshmen year and say, "coach I'm ready for you to move me up to the varsity". He would smile and say, "not yet Bo". That's what everyone had called me since I was a little boy, Bobo or Bo. It was a nickname given to me by my brother Chris. Chris is 11 months older than me. He was a sophomore and recently been moved up to the varsity. He was there. Running out of that dressing room and had even worked his way into a starting position. It made me want it even more.

I'm surprised Coach Roberts didn't put a restraining order out on me. I was bugging him every day and letting him know I was ready. Physically and skill wise I wasn't sure if I was ready for that action. The varsity competition was amazing to watch. My cousin Victor Spencer was a senior and star of the team as well as the area. He had played varsity since he was a freshman. I watched and admired him year after year. Larry Owens was my freshmen basketball coach. He ran and worked us as if he was upset with us about something. I'd ask him, "man coach why you running us so much and working us so hard"? He'd reply to me, "I'm just trying to get you ready Bo". Because of him, I felt my mind, body and soul developing. He pushed me harder than I had ever been pushed before. He ran us so much I forgot my foot was broken.

With six games left in the varsity regular season, Coach Roberts came to me and said I would be practicing with varsity and finishing the season with them. It was the happiest I had ever been. It was a dream come true. Finally, it was my chance. I didn't play much in the last six games. However, we made the playoffs. We lost but I got a chance to play and I scored my first eight points of my varsity career. The experience of running out in front of thousands of people was exhilarating. After growing up with my classmates and playing with them every year, I had finally made the separation I desired. I wanted to be different. I was different. I wanted the pressure. I wanted to lead. I wanted to be the best basketball player Lamesa had ever seen. I wanted to be big time.

The summer before my sophomore season was the most important of my life. I was officially a part of the Lamesa Golden Tornado basketball team and there was no going back. This was it. Every opportunity I had hoped and dreamt for. It was tough, because I had to learn to deal with longer harder work with the pain in my broken foot. But I wasn't going to let that hold me back. Coach Roberts had given me a chance and I was going to make the most out of it. I was going to build my own legacy. Therefore, I dedicated myself to my basketball more than ever before.

Younger brother Cedric in the background with the assist.

DEDICATION

Through the pain, I worked very hard on my body and my game. I was doing 1600 jump ropes a day to strengthen my legs and feet. I was running as much as possible and playing basketball as much as I could. Coach Roberts told me I had a chance to start as a sophomore so that made me work even harder. I worked harder that summer than I had ever worked before. Once school started, my maturity, growth and vision for what I wanted had grown. I was the only sophomore on the varsity. It made me feel special. Not because none of my friends were with me but because I had been in a lonely terrible place since 7th grade. Because of my opportunity, my grades began to get better. Because I was so caught up in my despair the past few years, I wasn't putting the effort into my classwork like I should have been. Coach Roberts gave me life. I also knew if I wanted to achieve my dream of playing college basketball, my grades would have to be better. I dedicated myself to be the best Jerry "Bobo" Mason I could be.

Once the season started, I had earned me a spot as a starter. I could tell all the work I had put in the past summer was paying off. I had increased my vertical jump to 42 inches from when I was a freshman when I could barely dunk. My brother Chris was the leader of the team, but I was the showman. I would bring the crowd to their feet with deep shot making, high rejecting blocked shots and thunderous dunks. No one could do what I could do. I was making the separation and setting a brand of basketball people in Lamesa had never seen. All because Coach Roberts saw something in me and gave me a chance. I knew he trusted me. He had to. The shots I would shoot from half court. The reverse dunks I would attempt during the games. It was unorthodox and something that could not be taught. It was me, Jerry Mason. It was my style. It was my game. It was my swag. Every kid deserves to have a high school coach like Wayne Roberts. Every kid deserves to have a coach who is willing to let them fail so that they may succeed.

We won district and made it to the playoffs. Once again, we lost our first game. It was devastating. I had a horrible game and felt responsible for our loss. It was a humbling feeling. It felt like we had let Lamesa and tradition down. My sophomore season was over. It was going so fast I remember after the loss, our news reporter coming to me and asking me what made me think I could make the shots I was shooting. He told me I needed to stay inside and stop hurting the team with my erratic shooting. Whether it was his intention or not, he hurt me deep. More than anything, he pissed me off. He motivated me to prove him wrong and I promised myself to never feel that dejected again. Coach Roberts being the great coach that he was, assured me that it wasn't my fault and that we were going to have a great next season. Before I continue my high school basketball journey, I want you to understand that without my coach trusting in me and giving me the opportunity, this journey would be over. However, as fun and overwhelming as my journey had been my freshmen and sophomore year, my final two years were magical.

Seeing something I wanted and going and getting it. Being creative in my own vision. Coach Roberts in the background letting me be me.

STATE BOUND

All summer we worked as a team to prepare for the next season. We were determined not to make it to state, but just not to get beat in the first round. It was my Jr. season and it was Chris' senior year. It was our best chance at making it all the way. We had achieved most if not all the individual accolades available to high school basketball players at the time. My life had changed drastically since I broke my foot in 7th grade. No one even paid attention to my limp. My basketball popularity had gotten so big, it caused the pain, doubt and fear I had back then to fade away. Well, not the pain, but it was worth it. Now that I was a Jr., our team consisted of a group that had played Little Dribbler All-Stars back when we were kids. We had grown up together and played so much basketball together, we knew we were going to be good. The problem was that when we were kids, my brother and I weren't the stars of this group. Some of the others developed faster and were better than we were. Once we all got to high school, everyone was split up. Now we were back together, but my brother and I had surpassed them all with basketball. Because of that, we started the season off 1-5. During this time, Coach Roberts never let us get down on ourselves. He also understood the dynamic of our friendship and our journey together. Even though he wasn't from Lamesa and wasn't present during our Little Dribbler and Jr. High years, he knew we were having problems with our identity. Being the understanding and smart coach that he was, he found a way to make us all feel primary in our role on the team. From that point we went on a roll as a team.

We won 26 straight games and made it to the state championship game. All the years I had dreamt of just playing on the varsity team. Never could I have imagined I'd be a major part of leading Lamesa to the state championships. Unfortunately, we lost in the finals 65-63. Three points away from being state champions. From a broken 7th grader to a 1st Team All-State player. All because my Jr. High coaches didn't give up on me. Because Coach Owens worked me like crazy. Because Wayne Roberts believed in me and gave me a chance. "COACHES". I finished my Jr. season averaging 23 points a game and 13 rebounds a game. My brother and I received numerous individual awards for the second consecutive season. We were rock stars. They called us the "Mason Combination".

1984 - 1985 Golden Tornadoes

District 2-AAAA Champion, Bi-District Champion, Area Champion, Region I-AAAA Champion, AAAA State Ru

w: Tony DeLaRosa, Rufus Hunter. 2nd row: Steven Roberts, Aaron Winn, Richard Diaz, Jerry Mason, Chris
lt, Jeff Brown. 3rd row: Head Coach Wayne Roberts, Gilbert Arredondo, Alex Martinez, Doug Warren, Kenneth V
rrama, Keith Bryant, Coach Larry Owens.

State runner up team. Coach Roberts (top left) gave me the opportunity. Coach Owens
(top right), got me in physical shape to be prepared for the opportunity.

Chris would receive a full basketball scholarship to San Angelo St. University. He was recently inducted into the San Angelo St. basketball Hall of Fame. The journey of us making it to state was a wonderful journey. I would love to take you through the journey game by game. It was fascinating. However, my main purpose for going through my journey is not to brag about me, my brother or Lamesa basketball. But to let you feel how this journey took over my soul. How the journey took over my mind. It consumed me. It consumed me way before Wayne Roberts was in the picture. It consumed me way before I broke my foot in the 7th grade. It consumed me when Coach Smith gave me that uniform back when I played Pee Wee baseball.

When I first started writing this journey, you may remember me saying I was addicted. I think we were all addicted. We loved and played all sports. All the time. Everybody has a different destiny. But the passion that sports provide is universal. It bridges gaps and builds bonds that will last forever. So many kids are consumed by sports at an early age. Some, like myself, may be addicted to them. The unfortunate thing is a lot of kids don't have a Coach Smith, a Larry Owens or a Wayne Roberts. Because of that, those kids will never have a journey. They will never have a story to tell or write. It's imperative parents that on all levels, you find that Wayne Roberts. I had my Wayne Roberts for one more season. It was the most exciting basketball year of my life. Although it wouldn't be the end of my basketball journey, it would be the last year I would be free to be Jerry "Bobo" Mason.

RECOGNITION

My brother and the rest of the seniors had gone off to college. I was finally the man. All those lonely nights I would cry myself to sleep in pain. All the doubt that rushed through my brain and took over my body. All the embarrassment because I walked different than everyone else. I just wanted to be normal. I just wanted not to hurt and to walk normal. All that I dreamed to be. All that I desired to be. All that I hurt to be. I never thought I would be the man. I never thought I would be considered the best basketball player to ever play at Lamesa High School. But I was. I felt I was. I knew I was. I can't really put into words how engulfed I was in this journey. I felt if it ever ended, I would be a nobody. I wouldn't know what to do without it. I felt I would die. It was who I was. I knew I had to be ready to shoulder the load my senior basketball season. I knew it was going to be extremely hard to win district again or have a chance to go back to state. I was going to be primary and everyone knew it.

We were going to have to start the season off with four new starters along with me. None of them had any varsity experience. It was going to be tough to maintain tradition. However, this moment is what I had always dreamt about. It was my responsibility to make sure no one took advantage of my young teammates coming up to varsity. One of them would be my younger brother Cedric. He was about to start his varsity journey as a sophomore. I had to protect and lead them. I had to allow them to experience what I had been allowed to experience. Lamesa Golden Tornado basketball. I was determined to make sure that there wasn't any player or team in the state could prohibit me from achieving my goals. I was determined to be the best basketball player in the nation.

During the summer before my senior season I began to receive basketball letters from a lot of colleges. They were expressing their interest in me attending their university on a basketball scholarship. It was a dream come true for me. I was being acknowledged and recognized for my hard work and perseverance. God was truly blessing me. I was receiving letters from colleges such as Seton Hall, Wyoming, Texas Tech, Wake Forest, UTEP, Texas A&M, Texas, San Angelo St. and Texas just to name a few. It was the most overwhelming moment and experience of my life. To make it even more special, Coach Roberts presented me with my first letter. The Coach that saw a skinny, broken freshman and gave him a chance. Unlike today, when I was playing Jr. High or high school basketball, there was no AAU or travel summer basketball. To be recognized and found in dusty Lamesa Texas, made it even more special and rewarding.

However, to finish off my summer, I traveled with a team from Lubbock Texas to play in the national BCI tournament in Phoenix Arizona. It was the first time I traveled out of the state of Texas. Not only would it be the first time I would travel out of the state, but it would be the first time I would play against teams from other states. It would be the first time I played against the best players from around the country. I knew I was one of the best in Texas, but I always wondered how good other players from other states were. We did not have the internet or state and national rankings when I was in high school. I always wondered if I could compete with them. If all the hard work, I had been putting in was enough. I said I wanted to be the best player in the nation. This BCI tournament would be my opportunity to get all my answers and prove I was one of the best in the country or the best.

During the tournament, we played teams from Houston, California, Minnesota, Arizona and New Jersey. It was an awesome experience. We did not win the tournament or every game. But I did win the trophy for leading the entire tournament in scoring average. I finished the tournament averaging 34 points per game. I didn't see every player there, but I knew I was the best player at that tournament. No one could stop me from scoring or doing anything I wanted to do. I had my answer. I could play with or against anyone in the nation and dominate like I did in Texas. It validated my work and my struggles. During and after the BCI tournament I began to get more scholarship offers from other colleges. It was unreal, humbling and breathtaking.

When I got back to Lamesa, Coach Roberts was one of the first I saw to talk to about my BCI experience. He said to me, "I'm happy for you Bo, but I already knew you were the best player in the nation. It just took the nation some time to find out". He was always so supportive and positive. He had no problem giving us our credit for what we had achieved and become. More than anything, he had no problem telling everyone else. That attitude from Coach Roberts is something not to take for granted. In my many years of coaching, I've seen so many coaches that will not let their players be primary in their own journey. I've seen so many coaches' that speak negative of their players to the players themselves and to other people. Coaches that don't promote their players. Coaches that prohibit their players from opportunities. They do this because they can and there is no accountability for their selfish hateful ways. It was a blessed and positive way to end the summer heading into my senior basketball season.

My younger brother Cedric on the left. Carl Pennington in the middle and me on the right. With Chris and the other seniors graduating, Carl and Cedric had to step up for us to continue our winning tradition. Leading them was my opportunity to showcase my entire arsenal.

With my cousin Victor gone from when I was a Freshman and my brother Chris leading us my Sophomore and Junior years, it was finally my chance to stand front and center. With Coach Roberts trusting and standing behind me, it led to an awesome Senior season.

ALL AMERICAN SEASON

Before my senior basketball season started and even though school had started, I took my first official college basketball visit. It was to University of Wyoming. Only five years previously, I was lost, confused, scared, scarred, broken, lonely, frustrated, hurt, hurting and basically a nobody. Now, I was visiting a major division 1 university. The separation was complete. I had become elite. I had earned elite. Everything about the Wyoming visit was amazing. The state was beautiful. The snow was beautiful. The mountains were frightening because I had never seen mountains and anything so close to the sky. But they were beautiful. Texas is flat land and Lamesa is cotton fields. The team, coaches, players and people of Wyoming University were great. I loved it. They loved me. They offered me a scholarship while I was there. I cried. Nobody knew because I was alone on my visit. I did not accept nor decline the offer. I let the coach know that I would be making my decision after my basketball season was over.

Visiting the University of Wyoming was also my first time flying on a plane. It was the most frightening thing I'd ever experienced. But I knew if I was going to be a college athlete and play professional basketball, flying was part of the journey. Notice, I said play professional basketball. I knew I was good enough. It had always been my dream. But now it felt like a dream I could really achieve. I just had to keep working and keep getting better. If you are wondering, we did not fly to Phoenix for the BCI tournament. Even though we were an inexperienced team, we had a great season. There were college scouts attending my games they could be present at. There were college scouts at my high school, all the time. There were college scouts at my parents' house. There were college scouts calling all the time. However, I didn't allow the college recruiting circus to stop me from being present for my team and teammates. We went perfect in district again not losing a game. We had a few teams in our district ranked in the top 20 in the state.

Andrews High School was one of the teams in our district ranked in the State. They were ranked in the top 10 all season. They only had 2 loses before playoffs. Both to the hands of us. I finished my high school career never losing a district game. Alex Martinez on the left and me on the right. Playing defense to get the win.

Individually for me, it was a great season. I scored over 40 points in a game 10 times my senior season. I never had a game less than 20 points my senior season. I scored over 1000 points my senior season and over 2000 in three years and 6 games on the varsity. I finished my senior season averaging 32 points, 18 rebounds, 5 assists and 4 blocked shots per game. I finished my high school as the leading scorer in Lamesa basketball history. I finished in the top 5 in rebounding and blocked shots in Lamesa basketball history.

Once the season was over and my Lamesa basketball journey had come to an end, I knew I had to start focusing on my recruiting. Because of the great season I had, my recruitment had grown. I had letters and offers from at least 70 colleges from different divisions. I really couldn't believe it. I couldn't believe how fast the journey had gone from my 7th grade until that moment. It was a blur. I couldn't believe all those colleges were coming from across America to watch me play basketball. Not only to watch me play, but to convince me to come play for their college. It was a dream come true, but a very exhausting and mentally draining experience.

To get away from it all at times I would go over to my friends' house to hang out and shoot baskets. His name is Bobby Garcia. We had become good friends in 6th grade, and it continued throughout high school. One day while Bobby and I were outside shooting baskets, my sister Monique, called for me. When I got to the phone, she told me mom told her to tell me I needed to come home. It was weird because they never called for me before. I was bothered because I thought something may be wrong at home. I told Bobby I would call him but that I had to get home. Once I got there, my mom said some man had called for me and that he would be calling back soon. I asked my mom why they would call me home to talk with another scout when I had left home to get away from that for a while? After she gave me a few choice words, she explained it wasn't a scout and to just wait for the call. About thirty minutes later the phone rang and I answered. He asked, "may I speak with Jerry Mason". I replied, "speaking sir". He stated his name and went to say, "we have been watching you all

NATIONAL HIGH SCHOOL ATHLETIC COACHES ASSOCIATION

In recognition of attainment of highest standards of prep basketball performance

JERRY MASON
Lamesa High School - Lamesa, Texas

Is hereby named

**National High School
BOYS BASKETBALL
ALL-AMERICA
1986**

Selected by
National High School Athletic Coaches Association

Sponsored by
CONVERSE ATHLETIC FOOTWEAR

Executive Director, NHS/ACA

National Sales Promotion Manager

When I received this honor and plaque, I was honored but didn't know the full magnitude of it. Only because I felt it was just the beginning and more honors of this magnitude were coming for me. I had no chance to achieve at Tech.

season. Congratulations on a wonderful senior season". I replied, "thank you very much sir". He went on to say, "we were very impressed by your basketball talent, consistency and leadership". He then said, "not only were we impressed with your basketball talent but also with you as a person."

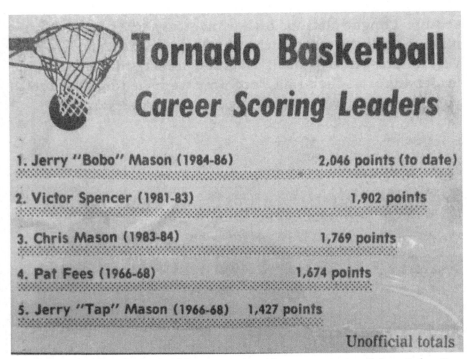

Tornado Basketball
Career Scoring Leaders

1. Jerry "Bobo" Mason (1984-86)   2,046 points (to date)

2. Victor Spencer (1981-83)   1,902 points

3. Chris Mason (1983-84)   1,769 points

4. Pat Fees (1966-68)   1,674 points

5. Jerry "Tap" Mason (1966-68)   1,427 points

Unofficial totals

Because Coach Roberts gave me the opportunity to become someone, I chose to be #1.

Even though I didn't know where he was heading, I once again replied, "thank you very much sir". Lastly, he said, "because of your outstanding season and accomplishments, our committee has selected you to the Converse All American Team. We only select two from each state and you are one of them". I burst into tears and said, "are you, serious sir. Wow, thank you all very much. It was my happiest day and the biggest honor of my life". He told me that my high school and I would be receiving All American plaques for the honor. I was blown away.

Once I got off the phone, I was shocked and at a loss for words. I told my mom what he said then she was excited for me. I couldn't wait to tell my family, friends and Coach Roberts. I wanted to tell him first because I appreciated so much what he had done for me. I called him and said, "guess what coach"? He said, "talk to me Bo". I said, "I got a call from a man and he said I was selected to the Converse All American Team". He replied, "well alright. Congratulations Bo, you earned it, you deserve it and I couldn't be happier for you. No one deserves it more than you". I told him thanks and if it wasn't for him believing in me as a freshman, I wouldn't have had this opportunity. I told him thanks for letting me grow the way I needed to grow. I told him thanks for letting me fail and figure it out before giving up on me. I told him thanks for trusting me to do the things I did. I told him thanks for putting faith in me to preserve his job which feeds his family. I told him thanks for allowing me to become Jerry "Bobo" Mason. I told him thanks for allowing me to build my own legacy through the rich tradition and legacy Lamesa basketball already had. It was truly an All-American Season. From a broken lost 7th grader to the first All American basketball player to ever play for Lamesa High School.

PRIZES WITHIN
THE JOURNEY

Once I earned my first All-star bid during Pee Wee baseball, I was hooked. I was hooked on the separation and the awards that came with it. I remember getting an All-star pen and an All-star hat for making All-stars in baseball. From that feeling, we all competed for All-stars, all tournament awards and most valuable player awards. Those awards made you a part of the elite and most valuable player made you elite. It was addictive. When I broke my foot in the 7th grade, I felt I would never be a part of the elite again. I for sure never thought I would be elite. I think that feeling will always have more impact on me than the feeling I had once Coach Roberts gave me my chance and all that I earned with it. I would not wish that devastating feeling on anyone. However, what a blessed high school journey I had. To experience so many great feats regardless of my adverse moments. From Pee Wee All-stars to basketball high school All American, because of great men and coaches. Here are my accomplishments and awards I received throughout my high school basketball journey:

Sophomore Season:

- 1st Team All District
- 1st Team All Region

Junior Season:

- 1st Team All District
- 1st Team All District
- 1st Team All South Plains

- 1st Team All Region
- 1st Team All State
- 1st Team All- Tournament Team @ State Championships

Senior Season:

- District 2-4A Player of the Year
- 1st Team All Region (MVP)
- South Plains Player of the Year
- TABC ALL-STAR- 3- point champion
- THSCA ALL-STARS (MVP)
- BCI Tournament- Tournament Leading Scorer
- 1st Team TABC All State
- 1st Team THSCA All State
- 1st Team Texas Sports Writers All State
- 1000+ Points in a season
- 2000+ Points in career
- Leading scorer in Lamesa basketball history
- 1st Team Converse American

I'm not bragging with presenting the awards. Everyone has a different journey. This just happens to be mine. But through my journey, I want to show kids, parents and coaches that anything is possible. That anything is possible if kids work and believe, that parents trust their instincts and that coaches sacrifice for the betterment of the journey. Athletes need coaches that listen, learn, assist and provide what's needed for each athletes' journey. These are things I was able to accomplish because Coach Roberts believed in me. He believed in me when I wasn't very good. He believed in me when I wasn't very strong. He believed in me when I had shown nothing for him to give me that opportunity. Coaches don't give up on your young athletes' so easily. They may not look, know or play the part at the time. But with your trust and positive energy, the broken soul can evolve into your All American.

FACTORS

Before I transition into my college journey, I want to point out things all kids and parents need to know.

From my playing days and coaching days, I've learned the major factors that can enhance or derail the journey.

The four factors I think are always involved in the outcome of the journey are:

1. Yourself
2. Parents
3. Peers
4. Coaches

If you'll look at your current situation or reflect on a situation or journey you went through, you'll realize one or more of these factors had an impact on the outcome. 1-3 of the factors don't even have to apply to sports outcomes. But in dealing with sports, #4, coach, is the most influential of them all. The outcome doesn't always have to be negative or positive throughout the journey. In sports, if you start in Pee Wee, Pop Warner and Little Dribblers, you will encounter a lot of peers and coaches throughout your journey.

The two constants are you and your parents. As the case in my journey, I had great coaches and mentors from Pee Wee baseball through high school basketball. Which provided me an opportunity for a positive and fruitful journey. Even if all the factors are great it doesn't mean your journey will lead you to high school All American, a college scholarship and a professional contract. But it does mean you will at least have the chance to be the captain of your own journey. When you know you are the reason why you succeeded or didn't attain your dream, it allows you to be at peace in your soul with the outcome. But when you feel or know one or more of these factors were instrumental in your journey and dream ending, life has never been the same for me.

The peer factor is so huge in Jr. High and high school, it's called peer pressure. Some kids would rather follow the lead of their friends instead of being the leader of their own journey. In Jr. High, kids are really trying to find themselves and peers are a big part of that journey. There are also positive peers as well. From my 7th grade season to my 12th grade seasons, my peers were very influential in my journey. When I made my mind up to sacrifice things to be the best basketball player I could be, some of the friendships I had faded. Even though some of us had the same dreams, we didn't have the same desire to achieve those dreams. Some of my friends preferred to party or drink but I preferred to work out. They felt I thought I was better than them and that caused friction in our friendship. I sometimes wanted to do things they didn't want to do and I to would feel about them as they did about me. I had to make tough decisions based on that, friends or dreams. It's a tough situation for kids who have been friends since youth sports to be in. Some choose the friends.

But if they are really friends, they wouldn't make you choose. They would be supportive in your desires and decisions as will you in theirs. That alone creates pressure between you and your peers. The yourself factor can be first or last on the list. It can be first because you can make your mind up early that you will let no one or nothing derail your journey. The younger the athlete, the more likely they won't be able to put themselves before the coach or parent factor. However, in my journey even though I had my mind made up I was in control, one factor interjected in my journey and another one ruined it. So, no matter where the yourself factor falls, it can be altered by parent, coach or peer pressure. Parents can be the worst or best factor during the journey. The most important component of that is that they are your parents. Because of that, they love you so much sometimes it blinds them to the things in the journey they need to see most. This was the case with my dad.

Him loving me, knowing my potential and trusting that alone would help me attain my dream, blinded him to the thing he needed to see the most. That thing is that ability and potential mean nothing if you don't have a coach that's willing to allow you to display your abilities to the fullest and is willing to allow your potential to grow. Even though I didn't want the college he wanted for me, because he was my dad, my yourself factor was altered. Because we love our peers, parents and coaches, we ourselves allow them to influence our journey. Sometimes for the worse. As you read my next journey, you will see how my dads' rationale affected my vision and led me to the wrong coach. These two factors, dad and coach, would ruin me and my soul forever. Here's my journey.

THE BIG APPLE

Trying to decide where to continue my academic and athletic career was very complicated, tiring, overwhelming and a journey within the journey. It amazed me that all these schools were offering me a chance to play collegiate level basketball. They all made their university sound like it was the perfect one for me. Being raised to be nice and respectful to everyone, I found the recruiting process hard because I didn't want to hurt any of the coaches' feelings. I felt I should feel blessed and honored to attend them all. But reality was, all I could choose was one.

It was like telling a girl that really wanted to date you that you weren't interested in dating her. But you were for sure going to date someone, just not her. It was tough. But at the same time, it was amazing!! I had already visited the University of Wyoming in the fall. At the time, nothing had compared to that. I went to visit Texas Tech University next. It was a drive visit away from Lamesa. I had watched Texas Tech play games a couple of times in person but more on television. Tech was a member of the Southwest Conference. It was a very competitive and great conference. The conference had teams nationally ranked from time to time during my time from Jr. High through high school.

Therefore, it wasn't a bad place to attend college and play basketball. However, it was just too close to home. After all the pain I had endured and everything that I had overcome, I wanted to go far away and play somewhere people had never heard of Lamesa. You could skip school in Lamesa, go to Lubbock where Texas Tech was located and be home before your parents got off work.

I felt I had earned the opportunity to go wherever my heart and excitement lead me. I wanted to be far away and alone like I was mentally in the 7th grade. But this time, lost and far away in basketball paradise. I loved the Big East Conference. It was always on television in Lamesa. Georgetown, Syracuse, St. Johns, Villanova, Seton Hall, U. Conn, Boston College, Pittsburg and Providence. Walter Berry, Mark Jackson, Harold Pressley, Rony Seikaly, Dewayne Washington and Reggie Williams. Lou Carnesecca, Jim Boeheim, John Thompson, Paul Evans, P.J. Carlesimo, Jim Calhoun, Jim O'Brien, Rick Pitino and Rollie Massimino. Legendary conference. Legendary Universities. Legendary Players. Legendary Coaches. I wanted to be a part of that conference in my soul. Watching the games on Sundays was unreal. The competition. The battles. The loud boisterous fans. The professional arenas they played in. It was intoxicating.

Luckily for me, because of my great journey and blessed achievements, one of the universities and coaches recruited me hard. Seton Hall University. P.J. Carlesimo. Wow! Like I stated early in my journey, we did not have summer tournaments or summer AAU basketball. For Seton Hall from the Big East to find me In Lamesa and want me to attend their university was a dream come true. Nothing against any of the other universities, they were all tremendous. However, this was the Big East. At the time, Seton Hall wasn't one of the top teams in the Big East. But when I would watch their games, there was never an empty seat in the arena. A lot of times I watched their games, they would play in the New Jersey Nets professional arena. A lot of the games played in the Big East were played in professional team arenas. The most famous was Madison Square Garden where the New York Knicks played their home games.

The thought of me, Jerry Mason, this broken foot kid from

Lamesa playing in the Big East in these legendary arenas kept me up all night. It consumed me. Coach Carlesimo was a cool man. He spent a lot of time in Lamesa. That meant a lot to me. I remember asking him if he really wanted me. His response was,

"I can recruit my area, Jersey, New York, Philly, Baltimore or wherever and find tons of players that would love to play at Seton Hall, Jerry". "But I'm all the way out here in the middle of God knows where because I want you".

Because I had once been so low and lost, it was hard to imagine or conceive that this was real. So, I set up my next visit to Seton Hall university. I asked coach where Seton Hall was located, and he said South Orange, New Jersey. I asked while I was visiting would I get to see New York City. He said it was a possibility and that was good enough for me. I was going to visit Big East Seton Hall and a chance to see the Big Apple.

COMMITTING

I remember leaving an All-star game from Houston Texas flying on my visit to Seton Hall University. I had my wish. I was alone, heading to basketball paradise. No one could imagine or comprehend the journey I was on. No one I knew had ever experienced a journey like I was blessed with. A journey I earned. Even when I tried to explain to people the magnitude of the things I was experiencing throughout the journey, the places I was seeing, words did it no justice.

Once I arrived and got off my plane in Newark NJ, I said to myself, "I'm home". The cold bitter air screamed basketball. The buildings. The people. The accents. It all screamed, "come to me Jerry Mason". Even before I made it to campus for my visit, I knew this is where I wanted to be. Once I arrived on campus, I felt so far away from everything. Home, my parents, my siblings, friends all seemed so far away. I felt new. I felt an obligation to represent for my family, Coach Roberts and Lamesa. I felt lonely. Not like I did when I was lost in my own in misery. Lost mentally in a place no one would understand because they would not or could not believe me. I was lonely in my new world. I was lonely in my new dream. I was lonely not because I wasn't surrounded by people but lonely because they weren't my people. I loved it. This is where I had to be. Seton Hall University.

I knew in that instance that I was going to be able to change my life and my families' life through this journey. I could feel and smell it in the air. It felt and smelled like opportunity for change. Opportunity for growth. Opportunity for greatness. Opportunity for Jerry Mason to rewrite history for Seton Hall basketball. I remember my chaperons being Mark Bryant and

John Morton. They were the stars of the team even though at that time, Seton Hall basketball was at the bottom of the Big East Conference. I remembered them from television. I couldn't believe I, Jerry Mason, was there with them. I remember John asking me in his Bronx voice, "Yo, where you from and why you so skinny son". I replied, "I'm from Lamesa a little town outside of Lubbock where Texas Tech is". He asked me while looking at Mark, "Yo why coach go way out there and bring this dude back? Yo, he must be good or something for coach to do that". I really didn't know if I was to respond or not, but I did anyway. I said, "he came way out there to bring me back here because I'm cold and no one can hold me at this basketball thing". He laughed and said, "yeah whatever, we gone see when we go ball son". I replied, "yeah we will". I'd love to tell you everything about my visit to Seton Hall.

Just know that everything about it was right and perfect for me. Mark and John even took me to Madison Square Garden to watch a game. Wyoming University was one of the teams playing. It was crazy watching guys you met on a visit to Wyoming playing in New York during my visit to Seton Hall. It was weird. Like a weird beautiful dream. We waited around after the game because John and Mark knew players from Wyoming. When they came out and saw me standing there with the Seton Hall players, Turk from Wyoming frowned and said, "yo what are you doing here in New York"? I gave him a dab and a hug and said, "I'm here visiting Seton Hall". He replied, "I thought you were going to come play with us, Seton Hall sucks".

Even though I knew in the core of my soul I was going to commit to Seton Hall I replied, "I'm just visiting". Once again, me being a nice boy or a coward, I didn't want to say too much and show I was leaning toward Seton Hall. Imagine my life. Alone in the middle of nowhere, New York City, and great basketball players from great universities wanting me to be their teammate. It was addicting. Something I never wanted to end. I was addicted to the separation. This was my opportunity to put Lamesa on the national map. A chance for me to be on tv playing in the Big East where kids from my town could see me and say, "if Jerry "Bobo" Mason can do it, so can I".

This was my destiny. This was my legacy. I said earlier, Coach Carlesimo was a cool man. He was also an honest man. He didn't sugarcoat and pretend and sell false dreams. He was a motivator, a visionary and medicine for a blessed but broken soul. He asked me honest questions and gave me honest answers. He asked me, "Jerry, what do you think your strengths and weaknesses are?" Once I explained to him what I thought they were, he responded like a great coach should. He made me understand that what I told him my weaknesses were easy fixes. That he would get me with the right people and make sure I'm comfortable in those areas.

But he also said to me,

> "Jerry, you're going to do things no one in the Big East has ever seen. You are going to be amazing".

Then he said to me something that I hear in my head and feel in my soul everyday still,

> "Jerry with you at Seton Hall, by the time you are a Junior, we will win a national championship".

I said,

> "aww come on coach".

He said,

"I wouldn't bring you way out here just to lie to you son. You just don't know how great you're going to be in the Big East and for us".

I was blown away. I was deeply touched he felt so much about my basketball ability. I responded saying, "thank you so much coach for the kind words and trust. I can do it. I want it coach. I'm committing to Seton Hall".

Not only was the air perfect for basketball, but Coach Carlesimo was perfect. Not one time did he say anything negative to me or discourage the opportunity for me to be great. He was a lot like Coach Roberts. Even though I know I had deficiencies like all high school players do, Coach Roberts never focused on them. He focused on the positive and what you could do. When I was talking to Coach Carlesimo and told him what I thought my weaknesses were, he immediately jumped to my positives and how great I was going to do because of them. Initially, I was committing to Seton Hall University because it was Big East basketball. But, after my visit, Coach Carlesimo was my number one reason for wanting to be a Seton Hall Pirate.

LIFE CHANGING DECISION

Once I returned home from my Seton Hall visit and told every-one who wanted to know how great it was, I told my parents and Coach Roberts that I had verbally committed to attend Seton Hall. It could only be a verbal commitment because national signing day had not arrived. A verbal commitment is not bounding, but for me I was bounded by my desire to be a Seton Hall Pirate. It was where I wanted to go, play basketball and start my new journey that would dictate the rest of my life.

My parents, Coach Roberts and everyone else was happy for me. It was a major accomplishment to be from Lamesa and now be able to attend college on a full athletic scholarship in another state. Also, in the top basketball conference in the nation.

Because I hadn't signed the letter of intent to attend Seton Hall University, I was still getting calls from many universities wanting me to visit. I still had official visits left that I could attend. I had taken some unofficial visits because they were in driving distance from Lamesa. Some of my peers were telling me to take the rest of my visits because I had earned the visits and they were free. They said I should take advantage and travel and see the world even though I had verbally committed to Seton Hall.

What they did not know is the visits weren't free. I didn't have to pay for the visits with money, but with my soul. I wasn't about to go and pretend to a university who thought a lot of me and wanted me to attend and I knew I wasn't going to attend. My soul wasn't made that way. I wanted to attend Seton Hall University and I had my mind made up. It was hard telling coaches that thought so much of me and my abilities that I had made my decision. However, it was the right thing to do. I was so happy. But more than being happy, I was relieved.

Even though I wouldn't have changed the blessing of receiving so many college opportunities, the process was hard and nerve racking. Hearing so many different coaches advocating for their university. Hearing so many reasons why I would be a great fit for their university. It was tough for me to believe a lot of the coaches because some made me sound like I was the next up and coming great thing in college basketball. It was hard to believe because I had once been in such a desolate place. Not only with basketball, but with my entire physical, mental and emotional soul. I was probably the worst Mason to ever play at Lamesa Jr. High. I didn't think I would have a basketball career at all once I broke my foot in the 7th grade. I felt I would never make the varsity for Lamesa.

Now here I was turning down opportunities to attend some of the best universities in the world not just best basketball universities. I was so humbled. I appreciated each coach and university that showed interest in me. From the Jr. Colleges through the major division one universities. I felt so blessed and I thanked God all day and every day for him blessing me to be Jerry "Bobo" Mason. I felt in my soul that Seton Hall was going to complete me. I felt Seton Hall University was going to provide me every opportunity I had ever desired or dreamed to achieve. It was going to provide me a chance to play basketball at the highest college level possible. It was going to provide me an opportunity to get a business degree and intern on Wall Street while getting my degree. It was going to allow me to build my legacy and stamp Jerry Mason in the Big East record books. It was going to provide me an opportunity to become a Big East all American and fulfill my dream of making the NBA and becoming an NBA hall of famer.

Yeah, that's right, an NBA hall of famer. I was that good. I was that confident. I was that blessed. More than anything, attending Seton Hall University was going to provide me the opportunity to open minds of other major universities to how good Lamesa basketball was. For them to get out the major cities and go to the small towns and find diamonds like me. Going to Seton Hall University was going to allow me to be a trailblazer and open doors for me and many more. It was the biggest decision I had ever made for myself. It was the biggest opportunity through God I had ever achieved for myself. I was 18 years old making life changing decisions and I loved it.

THE PARENT FACTOR

While I was waiting for national signing day to sign my letter of intent to attend Seton Hall University, I worked on my skills all day and night. I was making sure that when I got on campus, there would be nothing holding me back from attaining everything I desired. Everything had calmed down with the recruiting, coaches and phone calls. My mind and heart had moved on from the Jr. High heartbreak, the beautiful high school journey and on to Seton Hall and all the wonderful things I felt coming. I felt everything was what and where it was supposed to be.

Until one day I came home from working out and my dad threw me a curve ball a major league superstar couldn't hit. He called me into his room and asked,

"hey stud, what do you think about Texas Tech"?

I frowned in disbelief and asked,

"what do you mean what do I think about Texas Tech"?

He answered me by saying,

"what do you think about playing basketball at Texas Tech? It looks to me like they are changing their style and getting some really good players".

I said,

"I don't think about Texas Tech at all daddy, surely not playing basketball there. I'm going to Seton Hall". I continued saying, "Seton Hall is where I want to go play. I already committed and they know I'm coming. I don't want to go play for Texas Tech or anyone else dad. I want to go to Seton Hall".

During my senior season, my son Jeremy was born. He is one of the reasons choosing Seton Hall was so difficult. Him being young and the distance was hard to imagine. When I was on my visit, I contemplated how difficult it would be to be away from him and how I much I would miss of him growing while I was there. Every time I talked myself out of attending Seton Hall, my soul would tell me,

"Seton Hall is the right place Bo. You can do this and make this work for you and your baby".

I trusted my gut. I knew it was the right place. Also, Coach Carlesimo was aware of my concerns about being away from my son. He made it clear to me that they would do anything they could legally do to make sure the distance from him wasn't as far away as it really was.

It was nice to know he was sensitive to the situation and he cared. Seton Hall University was right for me in every aspect. However, for some reason my dad suddenly thought Texas Tech University was the best place for me and everyone involved in my journey. I was very upset with him and destroyed to even imagine Seton Hall not being the place I attended. My dad and I would go back and forth for a couple of weeks about his pros and my cons for me attending Texas Tech.

I felt like I was back in that mental state I was in while in the 7th grade. I felt lost and not in control of my destiny. Back then it was the pain controlling my present and destiny. Now it was my dad, making me feel like what I wanted and desired paled to what vision he saw for me. After weeks of going back and forth my dad made his last pitch for me attending Texas Tech. He said,

> "stud, if something was to happen to Jeremy, you'd be 4 or 5 hours away by flight. If you went to Texas Tech, you'd be an hour away by car. He could grow up watching you play. Your momma, me and everybody could get a chance to see you play stud".

He finished by saying,

> "I know you want to go pro. It doesn't matter where you go to college stud, no one can deny you. You are just that good bud".

I knew in my heart after that, I had to go to Texas Tech. Not because I wanted to. Because I had to.

I couldn't go against what my dad thought in his heart was best for me. He was my daddy. I asked him,

> "why did you let me tell this man and university I was coming knowing you felt that way daddy? How am I going to be able to call Coach Carlesimo and tell him I suddenly changed my mind and I wouldn't be attending Seton Hall University. When he knows and I know that Seton Hall is where I desperately want to be"?

He said,

> "just call and tell him stud. It's part of the business. Kids verbally commit and change their minds all the time".

So, I said ok and agreed to make the call.

I had not felt that pain that deep in a long time. I was devastated and heartbroken. I did not want to make that call. I did not want to attend any other university but Seton Hall. I did not want to play basketball in any other conference besides the Big East Conference. I felt my dreams and future vanish in my core. I didn't have one positive feeling go through me that Texas Tech could fill that void I had. That void that Seton Hall and Big East basketball could fill. But still, I made the call.

That curve ball my dad threw me and the phone call I made that night to Coach Carlesimo had me empty from that night until this present day I write my journey for you. I knew I was empty that night, but God I didn't know that the journey following the phone call and attending Texas Tech University would alter my life as a young man, a basketball player, a dreamer, a dad, a friend, an employee and as a human being for the rest of my life.

This is a prime example of how the "yourself factor" can be altered. I was 100% sure I was going to attend Seton Hall University. Then my dad came to me with his rationale. Because he is my dad and I respect his thoughts, I changed my decision and my "yourself factor" was altered.

THE PHONE CALL

I cried as I was making the call to Coach Carlesimo. I was hoping he did not answer or that before he did, my dad would come and make me hang up. But my dad didn't come in and Coach Carlesimo did answer. I proceeded to tell him what my dad and I had talked about and told him I'd be changing my mind and attending Texas Tech University.

He was caught off guard for sure. He could tell I was crying, and he asked me if I was ok. I told him no and that I still wanted to attend Seton Hall. But I told him the points my dad made were valid and that I was going to go ahead and do what my dad thought was best for me. I was torn apart inside. I knew he knew I wasn't 100% sure about my change but he didn't persist or pressure me. He asked if it would be ok if he called and talked with my dad. I was ok with him calling my dad and deep down inside I was hoping when he did, he would somehow convince my dad that Seton Hall was where I needed to be.

I waited in anticipation to hear from my dad or Coach about the phone call. I was waiting on my dad to call me in or Coach to call me back and say they both concluded Seton Hall was where I was going to go. Coach Carlesimo was the first to contact me. He said he had talked with my dad and there wasn't a change. He expressed his appreciation to me and wished me luck. He also went on to say if things didn't work out at Texas Tech to call him and if he could help me, he would. He was a great man and I appreciated his respect and concern for me.

After talking with Coach Carlesimo, I talked with my dad. I told him I had talked with Coach and that I was hoping the phone call would have changed things for me. However, my dad was persistent and consistent with his beliefs. He told me to trust him and assured me things would turn out good for me attending Texas Tech University. Later that evening I called Gerald Myers, Head Basketball coach at Texas Tech, and told him I would be signing with Texas Tech.

Although I was still upset and disturbed about my decision, I signed with Texas Tech University on national signing day. It was a great blessing and accomplishment to be signing at a major Division 1 university in top conference. But I wasn't feeling special or any different than any athlete that signed that day. It wasn't the Big East. It wasn't in another state. It was in the Southwest Conference 80 miles from my hometown. I wanted to get away and build a legacy in that conference. Nonetheless, a Texas Tech Red Raider I became.

I loved basketball more than anything. I was determined to make the most of my blessing and opportunity at Texas Tech. I played with two players in an All-star game, James Johnson and Steve Miles, that had committed to play basketball at Texas Tech as well. They were really good players and that made me feel better about Texas Tech having a chance to win a national championship. I only wanted to win and be the best.

Sean Gay was the returning Freshman of the Year in the SWC and would have three years to play with me and the other freshmen coming in. So, with the talent there and coming in, even though it wasn't Seton Hall and the Big East, I felt we had a great chance to take over the college basketball world.

Like always, I worked hard all spring and summer preparing for my next journey. I prayed every night that this journey would be as beautiful as Coach Roberts had allowed me to make it. I couldn't stand losing and not being the best basketball player people had ever seen. I thrived on not losing and being the best. My everyday life was based on how those two things were going. I desperately needed the opportunity to make Texas Tech a national champion and be the best college player in the country while doing so. With that mentality, off to Texas Tech University I went.

NEW CRUSHING BEGINNINGS

Attending Texas Tech University was my new beginning. Unlike my freshman year in high school, I was coming in as a known national basketball player. When I attended high school as a freshman, I didn't even know myself as a human much less as a basketball player. But I still wanted to be great at basketball.

During preseason of my freshman year at Texas Tech, I could tell this journey was going to be different than any of my other journeys. It didn't have anything to do with basketball, it had something to do with Coach Myers. He was different.

From youth sports through my high school journey, my coaches, even though they were the coach, never tried to make me feel inferior because they were the coach. Coach Myers was different. He had an aura about him that made me feel like he was happy to be in control of our journey. He didn't speak much of us doing things or getting better to attain bigger or better things. He made me feel like I should be lucky or blessed to be at Texas Tech. He made me feel like Texas Tech was the provider of my present. He made me feel like he gave me a scholarship instead of me earning a scholarship. He made me feel like I knew nothing about basketball and what he knew is what I had to know or else.

He was old school without the willingness to bend for the blessed. He had all the answers without a question being provided. I felt in my soul before the season started, he was going to crush everything about me. It was a horrible feeling that wouldn't go away. He was embedding negativity in us before we even started. He was building a foundation for his excuses based on the deficiencies he said we had instead of helping us fix those deficiencies if they were present. He wasn't very enthusiastic about us. If he was, it was hard to tell.

He always let us know that it wasn't high school basketball anymore. That we couldn't do the things we did in high school now that we were in college. When he'd say that, I'd think to myself,

> *"if we can't play basketball like we played in high school, how can we play? You recruited us based on what we did in high school and now it's not good enough for Texas Tech University"?*

He was very pessimistic. Honestly, I didn't initially know if it was

Steve Miles, Rodney Henderson, Greg Crowe and myself during picture day before my Freshman season. I felt at that point, basketball as I had felt it, played it and knew it, was over.

pessimism or if he was afraid to be irrelevant. If he was afraid to be a part of our journey instead of controlling our journey. He planted negative seeds to control the narrative. Our supposed deficiencies were his scapegoat when things got tough, and had the possibility of reflecting on the great Gerald Myers.

His word was law and we had to abide by the law. He let us know that from the beginning. I was very disturbed by his domineering ways. I didn't go to Texas Tech to be changed or tamed or controlled. I came to win, get a degree and continue my journey I had earned with God's blessings.

I called my dad and told him before the season started that I didn't want to be there. I told him that Coach Myers was all about himself and not about the players. I told him,

> *"daddy, I don't want to be here. It's*
> *not going to end up good".*

But my dad wasn't hearing or believing what I was saying. He kept saying,

> "you've got to give the man a chance stud. The season
> hasn't even started yet. I think everything is going to
> be better than you think".

I said to him angrily,

> "dad, this isn't something I'm thinking, this is what I
> know and what I feel".

But my dad was persistent with his belief and told me to stick it out and see how it goes. Therefore, I did.

It was a crushing reality to the beginning of my new journey.

Coach Roberts would say to me, "Bo, I feel very lucky to be your coach, you are great and only going to get better from there". Coach Carlesimo said to me, "Jerry you are going to be great here at Seton Hall. You are going to do things these people have never seen. With you here Jerry, we can win a national championship". Coach Myers said to me, "you're going to have a hard time playing here because you can't play defense".

I could have been one of the best players he ever had. But he would have to let me do it my way. However, my way was unorthodox. My way was a way that couldn't be taught or contained. My way was more extraordinary than he had ever had. Therefore, in order to contain my greatness, he tried to embed in me I couldn't play defense. I was a winner and had always won. Winners don't win without playing defense. I'm a winner. When he'd say that, I'd think,

> "if I can't play defense, I just didn't walk on to Texas Tech campus and now I can't play. If I can't play now, I couldn't play defense in Lamesa. So why would you come recruit me and interfere with my plans to attend another university if you didn't like my defense?" "Why you come get me just to degrade me?" "Why you come get me and want me to be a lesser version of who I was when you got me? Why come get me to belittle me?"

Coach Myers didn't want stars, he wanted puppets. The problem was I wasn't a puppet for no one. Because of the great coaches I had up to that point, I was able to be Geppetto and be the puppet master of my own destiny. He wanted me to be like he was when he played. But I wasn't him and no one was me. I was different. I was a blessing from God for people who loved amazing basketball. I could do things no one could do. But because he had me, he had the ability through my love for basketball to control me. I had to do what he told me do in order to have a chance to play. I loved basketball more than anything in the world besides God and family and I just wanted to play it. So, if I had to be his puppet just to get an opportunity to fulfill my addiction, so be it.

As I stated earlier in my journey, I was addicted to basketball. I was addicted to winning. I was addicted to the crowds and the way they reacted to the way I played. I was addicted to being, the best. Coach Myers knew that. But instead of wanting to help me with my addiction, he wanted to change and control it. He wanted his addiction which was to control and manipulate to be my addiction. He wanted to be my Geppetto and me his puppet. What a horrible person to be as a coach. Knowing that kids you recruit have dreams to continue playing basketball after college in some professional capacity. But you bring them in and tell them they aren't professional material because the way they play basketball isn't good enough. Therefore, you try to control and change them to conform to your mediocre attitude of what you think basketball and greatness is. "Why come recruit me sir? Why come bother me sir?" "If I'm not good enough and you have to take me through a metamorphosis to play for you, WHY COME GET ME"?

Same picture from my high school journey. Defense is pride and effort. Defense is a desire not to lose. Defense is being a winner. I'd always had pride, effort and a desire not to lose. More than anything, I had always been a winner. I will always resent Coach Myers for trying to discredit those attributes in me.

THE COACH FACTOR

I didn't play much my Freshman year. Every day was a grind for me. He had already planted the seed in me and for the public for why I wasn't going to play much. He said I had to work on my defense. I didn't even know he recruited me for my defense. I thought he recruited me because I was a winner. I thought he recruited me because I was one of the top players in the nation. I thought he recruited me because I was one of the top scorers, rebounders and shot blockers in the nation several months ago. I thought he recruited me because I was a National basketball First Team All American.

I didn't know he recruited me to Texas Tech almost 80 miles from my hometown to tell me I suck and sit me on the bench. I didn't know he recruited me to Texas Tech to hold me accountable for fans sending him hate mail because he wasn't playing me. I didn't know he recruited me to Texas Tech to crush my dreams.

All the pain I had endured. All the loneliness, heartache, fear and depression I had to overcome. To overcome to get to a point where I earned an opportunity to get a basketball scholarship to go somewhere to continue growing and getting better. Somewhere to hopefully help launch me to the next level. Yet, here I was at Texas Tech University with a coach that thought so little of me. Thought so little of my struggles to get where I was. He never knew my struggles because he never cared to ask me. He never talked with me in Lamesa. I don't think he ever came to Lamesa. He wasn't in my high school hallways like the others who recruited me. He didn't even want me. He just didn't want anyone else to have me.

So, there I sat on his bench for almost an entire season. I played sparingly in some games, but most games I didn't play. I was 16-49 in field goal attempts my freshman year with a total of 57 points, 13 rebounds and 8 assists. This was for the entire season. Just under a year prior to my freshman season at Texas Tech, I scored over 1100 points, had almost 600 rebounds and over 100 blocked shots in just my senior year alone in high school.

I graduated from Lamesa High School in May of 1986. I started my Texas Tech basketball career in November of 1986. During that time, I went from one of the top basketball players in the nation to a kid sitting on the bench 80 miles down the road. But, if I would have attended Seton Hall University 1,000 miles away from my hometown, this same kid could help lead them to a national championship?

Coaches and their belief in you can help you change the world or their lack of belief in you can ruin your world. I was ruined from that experience. Sitting on that bench changed me. I was bitter, hurt, embarrassed, broken, pissed and humbled. This was what it must have felt like for some of my friends in 7th and 8th grade to make the B team when they knew they had A team abilities.

Even though Coach Myers hated my fans sending hate mail in support of me, it was one of the things that kept me going. They knew what I could do. They believed in me. They knew the real Jerry "Bobo" Mason. But all I could hear in my head was Coach Myers saying you can't do this, and you can't do that. He was basic and I was anything and everything but basic. I didn't know how to change or make myself conform to being basic. I didn't know how to do basic.

Coach Myers and I were just a conflict. He wasn't going to

change, and I couldn't change. The problem was, I loved basketball and I just wanted to play. What hurt the most is that we played top universities with top players my Freshman year and I had to sit and watch most of it. We played Kentucky who had Rex Chapman who was also a Freshman and he started for them. We played Kansas who had Danny Manning. We played Arizona who had Sean Elliott, Steve Kerr and Judd Buechler. It hurt so much because I knew I could play with those guys. But because I couldn't play defense in his eyes, I watched from the bench.

No matter what was going to happen next in my basketball career or regular everyday life, I would never be the same after my Freshman Texas Tech basketball experience. I was so happy when the season ended. Not because I didn't want to play basketball anymore but the experience and pain, I felt deep hurt too much.

I talked with my dad once again after the season about me transferring to another university to pursue my career. I wasn't even thinking on pursuing pro dreams at this point anymore. I just wanted to be somewhere someone believed and trusted me. I just wanted to be somewhere where a coach would allow me to be me and allow me to help a program continue to or begin winning. But again, my dad was persistent in his belief that the next years were going to be better.

Coach Myers and his assistants knew I was unhappy about the way he handled my Freshman situation. It was like he wanted to take the local area star and show people I was way smaller than the credit I earned from them. It seemed very hateful to me. Very dictatorship like. I despised him for that. It was his program and he didn't owe me the opportunity. But why come convince my dad of your intentions to convince me to come if you knew you had no intentions for me at all?

I'm not saying Coach Meyers was a plantation owner. But my definition of enslavement is having something or someone as your property and not allowing it or them to be free to explore the opportunities they desire. Especially when it's your responsibility to help them. But instead you choose to expose them and belittle the abilities they do have in order to focus on deficiencies you think they have. Furthermore, you use that rationale to prohibit them from prospering. ENSLAVEMENT. That's not a race, color or creed thing. That's a real thing.

This is my journey, but it happens to millions of athletes across the globe. Coaches using their responsibility to help athletes as opportunity to control them. But if administrations and presidents of universities are not going to hold the coaches accountable for the betterment of all their athletes, it's going to continue to happen.

Instead of Coach Myers benefiting from all the things I could do to help the team, he chose to utilize his excuses or beliefs about me to hold me down. I thought that was very selfish. There were players I grew up watching, respecting and playing against in my hometown that were way better than some of the opponents Texas Tech played. But you sit me and make me feel I'm inferior to these players? I saw him as a bigger fan of our opponents than of us the players he had. He would always tell us how good other teams and players on those teams were and tell us how bad individually we were. Very backwards and pessimistic. He seemed more like a movie critic to me than a coach at a major university with players life dreams in his hands.

My dad was convinced it was going to get better. The coaches even told me that the next year would be better. But I knew it wouldn't. I knew after my Freshman season we had a lot of seniors leaving and I would get more minutes. But I didn't dream to come to Texas Tech and get minutes by default. I had earned everything God blessed me with. I didn't need hand-out minutes from Texas Tech University. I knew the minutes, points and everything would get better. But how could they not when you did nothing your first year. They'd get better by default. But mentally and emotionally, the damage had already been done.

I knew no matter what because of the style and mentality of Coach Myers, the basketball wasn't going to be better. I knew people who had only heard of me and my basketball but were excited to see for themselves, would only see 10% of who I really was. They weren't going to see all the exciting things I could do with a basketball and on a basketball court. They were going to think, "is this it? What was all the hype about? An All American and he can only score 57 point in a season at Texas Tech. What a waste of a scholarship". The damage was done. Knowing if I stayed at Texas Tech, basketball as I loved and played it was over and it was a sickening feeling.

But it wasn't as easy to transfer out like it is today. Plus, my dad wasn't having it because he believed them when they told him, "things are going to be better and Jerry's going to do good here." SMH. Whatever COACH.

Where the bigotry was for me was you sat me on the bench because my defense was bad. Which meant all the players you were playing in front of me were good defenders. However, we didn't win our conference or make it to the NCAA tournament nor the NIT. So how good was their defense or better yet was I really that bad? Come on COACH.

In my years of coaching, I've always felt it was a blessing to be coaching each kid. No matter of their talent level or the things they could or could not do. It's a blessing to try and assist in the dreams of each player. The thing with Coach Myers was he didn't feel blessed to have me. If he did, I sure didn't feel it from him. It's his responsibility to make his players feel it. I felt he felt we should be blessed to have him. But he wasn't the prize in the crackerjack box, we were. I was. However, he had to be the prize and if things didn't go right, we were the bad crackerjacks. Regardless, I stayed at Texas Tech University. Here's the rest of my journey.

ROLLERCOASTER YEARS

Like I knew it would be, my Sophomore basketball season at Texas Tech was better than my Freshman season. I started some games and played some good minutes in more games than I did as a Freshman. However, I felt as if I was a shell of the basketball player I was in High School. I loved playing but the excitement level wasn't as high as I was used to it being. It was weird. I felt the Big East basketball excitement or the fans of basketball in the Big East was always present and electric.

Just being able to be on the floor and play was a good thing for me. But, being prevented from doing the things that made me who I was before coming to Texas Tech was suffocating. I wanted to be free and I wanted to do more. But I knew if I did, Coach Myers would sit me on that bench again. So, I did what I had to do to do what I loved to do. Which was play basketball. Even though I wasn't playing no way close to my full ability and potential, I was getting a chance to play.

The reason I put the emphasis on basketball season earlier was that everything didn't get better. Even though my basketball season had gotten a little better, a lot of other things in my life began to go backwards. I had always gotten descent grades starting with my Sophomore year in high school. I wanted to be recognized for more than just my basketball ability. But my desire to do well in class was tied to desire to continue to play basketball. The basketball was more primary in my soul than the academics. But the academics were important to me because of the basketball. So even though the minutes, points and rebounds got better, the BASKETBALL wasn't better.

There were no opportunities tied to the basketball. Coach

Myers had let us know that none of us were pro potential basketball players. It was crushing to hear him say that because that's what we all dreamed to be. So, I felt, "why am I here? Why am I busting my butt every day to get nothing but the opportunity to say I played at Texas Tech University? That wasn't my dream." Because of his words and my knowing, my grades began to plummet. I skipped classes often and my GPA dropped from 2.8 after my Freshman year to 1.7 after my Sophomore year. I began to turn to other things to fill the void in my heart and hide the pain in my soul.

If Coach would have believed in me, no one could have stood in my way.

I began to party more than going to class. I began to spend more time with women than I did at the Rec center working on my game. Coach Myers was never going to let me be great again. He was never going to let me showcase the real Jerry Mason to the college world. He had convinced my dad I was the problem. So, he could treat me and my dreams any way he wanted. He was Geppetto and I was his puppet.

It was very immature of me to go down that road. The things I did only affected me in the long run. However, at the time, that's what Jerry Mason needed for his sanity and peace of mind. I don't think Coach Myers ever thought or cared about the negative impact he had on me. I don't believe he ever cared that he was hurting me. He just had to be the reason things were good and blame others when things were bad.

There was no accountability for winning or greatness at Texas Tech. He never discussed winning a conference or national championship with us. He focused on the small victories he could attain by controlling the narrative. He punished us when we lost but never allowed us to control the winning. When we won, he was Gerald Myers the head coach. When we lost, we were the incapable athletes making a mockery of Texas Tech. It was a horrible atmosphere.

If it weren't for my teammates being there and going through some of the things with me, I don't know if I would have continued playing basketball. But I wasn't going to coward out on them and plus I still loved playing basketball.

I finished my Sophomore basketball season with 271 points, 45 rebounds and 35 assists. I was 100% better than those numbers and could have done so much more for coach and Texas Tech. But it would have meant he would have to change and let go of the reigns. That wasn't going to happen. I was just hoping that somehow, I could continue to get better and impose my blessings on Coach Myers and the rest of the basketball world. I had so much more beautiful basketball in me I wanted to display to the world. But Coach Myers wouldn't allow me to. I would pray every night and ask God why?

That jumper was money for sure. I guess Coach had enough because he was reluctant to take mine.

This is where I was with my life and basketball. Basketball was my life. I could see and feel it fading away right in front of my eyes. The bad thing is, there was nothing I could do about it. I was in too deep. Even if had the opportunity to leave Tech I felt I hadn't done anything or enough where any university would want this version of Jerry Mason. I decided to walk on faith and finish at Texas Tech.

My boy Sean Gay with the assist. He and I made a tough duo.

BEST SEASON

My Junior season at Texas Tech was my best basketball season and my best year since leaving high school. It was best because I finally decided to go with the flow. I had come to peace with my reality. That was, it was going to be hard to continue basketball after my Tech career ended. I wasn't happy about my acceptance, but it was better for my mental. I realized that Coach Myers wasn't going to change, push or encourage me to pursue greatness at Texas Tech in order to achieve greatness afterwards. But I also felt all I could do is what I could do. I knew I would never get a chance to showcase my true basketball potential and ability while finishing at Texas Tech. It was a humbling reality but again, it was the only way emotionally I could survive.

With that understanding, it gave me piece of mind and allowed me to progress forward. It was the first time I had took a pessimistic approach or outlook on my dream to be an NBA player. In the back of my mind, I kept hope that things would work themselves out and the opportunity would present itself. We had a talented team my Junior season. We had spurts during the season where we won multiple games straight. That gave us hope for finally making a post season tournament, but we fell short again.

I finished my Junior season with 337 points, 77 rebounds and 64 assists. Once again, they were disappointing numbers in my eyes because I knew how much better I could produce. Before coming to Tech, I had never not made the playoffs. We never lost a district game during my tenure on the Lamesa varsity team. We won district every year I played varsity. In Coach Myers eyes, I wasn't a good defender. What he should have been focusing on is that I was a winner. Don't recruit what you don't like sir, recruit what you need. It was the image he wanted portrayed of me to the public and the people. It was his ally to keep me crippled and not take him out of his comfort zone as a coach.

However, all he did was prevent Texas Tech basketball alumni and fans from viewing one of the most talented basketball players to ever play. He prevented me from having a chance to show my son greatness as he got older. He prevented me from an opportunity to achieve awards in the SWC. He prevented me from being able to put my name in the Texas Tech record books

I loved everything about basketball. Especially putting on a dunk show.

as one of the greatest to ever play there. He turned me into mediocrity and that will get you nowhere when you're trying to progress somewhere. Coach Carlesimo told me on my recruit visit to Seton Hall University that during my Sophomore or Junior season with me playing for Seton Hall we would win a national championship. During my Junior year at Texas Tech, Seton Hall lost on last second free throws in the national championship game to the Michigan Wolverines. I called my dad after they lost and said, "did you see the national championship game dad? That could have been me on that stage and I know with me they would have won. You should have just left me alone and let me go where I wanted to go. But instead I'm here and we haven't won conference and this man could give a crap about me or anything that has to do with me."

I was very upset with him. After a few seconds of silence, he responded, "yeah stud I saw it and I thought about you and the situation the entire time. I could see you out there putting on a show." I responded, "yeah, but I'm not. I'm here sitting doing nothing like I've done here for three years. Bye dad." I wished that I could have called Coach Carlesimo to apologize again, congratulate him and thank him for being honest and positive with me. But I'm sure I was the last person on his mind and the last he would want to talk with. So, I moved on thinking every day, what could have been. The last and most important college basketball game of the year. Every basketball fan and NBA scout scouting the talent, and I wasn't there. I was crushed.

Everything that I had felt in my soul when I first got to the Seton Hall University Campus was correct. It was the best place, conference and opportunity for me to win and pursue an NBA career. My two chaperones, John Morton and Mark Bryant, were both drafted in the 1st round of the NBA draft. Mark was the #21 pick in the 1st round and John was the #25 pick in the 1st round. Seton Hall was the right place. The Big East was the right conference. To add to that, everything I had felt about Texas Tech basketball in my soul before I attended was correct as well. We didn't attend or win any post season tournaments. Nor did any player I played with get drafted in any round into the NBA. Not even me. As I had stated earlier, we had a talented team my Junior season. In our top six player rotation we had a high school state champion, a state runner-up, high school All Americans, a Jr.

Inside or out. No matter where I was on the court. No matter what level of basketball. No matter what town, state or country. Nobody could stop me from getting buckets. No one could leave and not be impressed by basketball blessings.

college national champion, BCI national champions and winners. We had great talent and we all had won. For some reason collaboratively at Texas Tech, we all became average players and lost more than we won. Maybe I'm just fishing here or maybe there is truth to what I know and had experienced.

Coaches are the mediators to winning, greatness and dreams. Coach Roberts told us we would win. Then he allowed us to do it. Coach Carlesimo knew that Seton Hall would win. He told me so. Then, he allowed them to do it. Coach Myers told us how we should and could not shoot. Where we should go and not go. When to shoot and not shoot. He controlled everything. He never said we would win. He only told us the ways we would lose. So, we were robots for his vision of us and we lost.

Once I was able to stand the pain from my broken foot, I work extremely hard to become the athlete I became. When Myers gave me the chance, I showcased my blessings. Fans loved it. I loved it. Coach Myers felt it was unnecessary. Crazy.

FINAL NAIL IN MY DREAMS

Before heading into my senior season in high schoo I knew what was expected of me and I knew I was prepared for the expectations. I knew that after my senior high school season I would be attending college. I just didn't know where. I knew we had lost a lot of talent the previous season, but I knew with the work I had put in, I could continue our winning tradition. Heading into my senior season at Tech, I didn't know what to expect for me and for the team. I knew we lost some good players from last season's team, but I didn't feel the expectation was for me to step and be primary. I wanted the responsibility of being the number one option, but I didn't expect Coach Myers would allow me to be as free as I needed to be to get the job done. I knew it was my last basketball season, but I had no idea what was to come after the season.

I hoped my senior season would go great and the team would do well. I knew if I didn't do great things and the team didn't win, my chances of playing professional basketball were slim. Unfortunately, the season didn't go well. I had an injury that caused me to miss some games, but the accumulation of four years of negativity, mind games and dislike had taken its' toll. In my career I had never missed games and it would have killed me inside to do so. During the games I missed that year, it didn't hurt me as much as if I would have missed games in high school. I still loved basketball and that's why it bothered me missing games. But I didn't feel as important and needed to Texas Tech as I did when I played for Lamesa High.

I knew missing games wouldn't help my cause when wanting to play professional basketball. I also knew the body of work

I had over my four seasons at Tech wouldn't have pro teams knocking my door down. All I was hoping for was a chance to showcase my talent to any NBA team that would watch me. I finished my Senior season with 221 points, 46 rebounds and 36 assists. All numbers worse than my Junior season. I knew I would need help and or a good reference from Coach Myers to continue my basketball dreams. Knowing that, I felt the final nail being nailed into my dreams.

I never thought I could feel as low as I did in 7th grade when I broke my foot. But the reality of my career most likely being over, took my lowness, loneliness and depression to an unbearable low. 886 points, 181 rebounds, 143 assists and 30 blocked shots in my basketball career at Texas Tech University. I played an average of 18 minutes per game during my Tech career out of 40 minutes in a game. 22 minutes per game I sat there watching the game I loved and knew I could dominate. Knowing that within my 18 minutes I played I was going to be a shell of the player I really was. 22 minutes being a spectator and 18 being a puppet. I don't know which affected, changed, hurt or destroyed me the most.

2,100 points, 1,400 rebounds, 200 blocked shots and 250 assists in my Lamesa high school career. One of the top 150 basketball players in the nation coming out of high school. All the work, pain and sacrifices to be treated like mediocre help. The thing that hurts the most is that there is no accountability for coaches like Coach Myers who come in every practice or game day to kill the passion players have inside them. To kill the dreams and aspirations players have in them. Coach Myers never once thought about changing. Even when we lost, instead of reassessing his talent and make the necessary changes, he blamed us. He coached us and treated basketball like it was the 1970's when he started coaching at Texas Tech.

He knew when he recruited me, I dreamt of and had the ability to play in the NBA. But he had no intentions of helping me get there. It seemed to me he spent more time trying to prohibit the opportunity then enhance it. I think what Coach Myers and other coaches fail to realize or don't care to entertain is that even though we are college basketball players, we are still kids. Young men who have endured many negative things in their lives before they get to college. Young men who have overcome adversity in one or many situations. Young men who have work tremendously hard before, during and after adverse or terrible incidents. Young men who have dreams during and because of these tough times. Young men whose dreams consists of happiness, more prosperity than adversity and taking care of their families. Young men who just want a coach to put themselves second in their dreams. A coach who will trust in them and who they were before they got to college. A coach who will wake up every day to assist to the best of his abilities in assisting in making or helping the dream come to fruition.

As I stated during my journey, defense is effort and pride. It's not perfect, but it's a desire win no matter what it takes. No bucket for him or many others no matter what Coach Myers wanted people to think. Nothing for nobody. Period.

Not a coach who's already blessed to have lived his dreams and blessed to be a college head coach. Not a coach who has these blessings but still has to be the primary benefactor in his players dreams and journey. Not a coach who knows he should change for the betterment of his players abilities but refuses to out of spite or hate.

I consider being in love with sports and the moments sports provide to be like tattoos. Those moments good, bad, great or mortifying, are etched into your soul and your brain. Some are very painful and sometimes impossible to remove. Some turn out to be beautiful pictures and others you wish had never happened. They are our memories and are things we will never forget. The moments and memories we create for ourselves through sports brand us for life. I was branded from my Pee Wee years playing for Jones McCall Pharmacy. I was a 1st grader and those moments are etched into my brain and I remember them like it was yesterday. Tattooed in my soul forever.

Parents don't think just because it's tee ball, pop warner or Little Dribblers that there won't be an impact embedded into your kids from the journey. It may be a negative or positive impact or both. They will remember, feel and live it for the rest of their lives. It will be their relevance in their present when they are remembering their past. Know that a positive and understanding coach can make those everlasting tattoos beautiful visions.

It doesn't matter when you start your athletic journey or in what sport, the coach is going to be a major component of how that journey turns out. Even if your child is not the most talented or gifted in the sport he or she loves, the coach can still make it a wonderful journey. Being positive, a good teacher and reinforcing has nothing to do with the DNA of an athlete. When a coach alters his responsibilities as a coach based on how good or how bad a kid is, that coach is not the right person for any journey.

Remember, COACH is a title that should be earned. If a person is not going to teach, learn, assist, enhance, believe and help fulfill the journey, he or she shouldn't be called COACH. Throughout my college basketball journey, I called Gerald Myers Coach the entire time. However, he was more like a dominant boss. But because he was the Head Basketball coach at Texas Tech University, Coach is what he was called by default. However, I don't feel he was there to help fulfill my journey or dreams. I can't think of many things he taught me while I played for Texas Tech that benefited me as a basketball player or as a young man going out into the real world. I was like one of his employees passing through one of his job lectures. During that lecture he spent the entire time telling me how good his program was, how good he was and how unsuited for his program I was. I should have called him BOSS instead of COACH.

Unfortunately for me, like my youth sports, Jr. High and High School journeys, my college and Texas Tech journey will be tattooed in my soul forever. It just happened to be the biggest and most important journey of my life. My final journey before starting the earned and most fun and productive journey of my life.

Parents make sure your kids final tattoo isn't painted by someone who doesn't care how the art comes out. The pain, loneliness, disorientation, embarrassment, shock, thoughts, regrets, fear and disappointment stays embedded in my soul. It had consumed and consumes my every thought, mood and feeling of everyday. 34 years later I still ask the same questions in my head every day.

Yeah, I dunked. Yeah, I shot that ball well. But I played harder on defense than anyone. Coach Myers words didn't match my effort or record, until I played for him.

IF I HAD TO DO IT ALL AGAIN

IF I HAD TO DO IT ALL AGAIN, WOULD I MAKE THE SAME

MISTAKE?

IF I HAD TO DO IT ALL AGAIN, WHICH OPTION WOULD I TAKE?

IF I HAD TO DO IT ALL AGAIN, COULD I AT LEAST MAKE AMENDS?

IF I HAD TO DO IT ALL AGAIN, WOULD I MEET SUCH WONDERFUL

FRIENDS?

IF I HAD TO DO IT ALL AGAIN, WHERE WOULD I BE TONIGHT?

IF I HAD TO DO IT ALL AGAIN, WOULD I AT LEAST DO SOMETHING

RIGHT?

IF I HAD TO DO IT ALL AGAIN, WOULD I ALLOW MY DAD TO HAVE HIS

SAY?

IF I HAD TO DO IT ALL AGAIN, WOULD I DISOBEY HIS WISHES AND DO IT

MY WAY?

IF I HAD TO DO IT ALL AGAIN, WOULD I HAVE ONE SON INSTEAD OF

TWO?

IF I HAD TO DO IT ALL AGAIN, WOULD I EVEN BE WRITING

TO

YOU?

IF I HAD TO DO IT ALL AGAIN, WOULD I FEEL SO LOW, LOST, HURT AND

DEFEATED?

IF I HAD TO DO IT ALL AGAIN, WOULD I AT LEAST FEEL I MY HEART THAT I

TRULY COMPETED?

IF I HAD TO DO IT ALL AGAIN, WHILE IN COLLEGE WOULD I TAKE A

DIFFERENT APPROCH?

IF I HAD TO DO IT ALL AGAIN, I'D BE HAPPY AND FULFILLED DEEP IN MY

SOUL BECAUSE I'D CHOOSE A DIFFERENT COACH?

"BROKEN"

As I am writing this journey, it will have been 30 years since I last played basketball for Texas Tech University. I had a few CBA tryouts and a couple of free agent camp tournaments, but no help from Coach Myers. If you don't have a great college career, it's hard to get teams to take a chance on you. I needed help and a reference from my college head coach. Nothing. He spent so much time trying to convince the public, media and myself how bad I was. But when he had a chance to step and speak highly of who he knew I truly was and my talents, he disappeared.

Nevertheless, I had a few opportunities to go play professional overseas but that wasn't my dream. It was consolation to my dream and at that time I was emotionally destroyed. I still loved basketball, but I didn't love it enough to chase the dream via playing overseas. My confidence was shot. My pride was challenged. My soul was empty. The only option I wanted was to play in the NBA. If I didn't feel before I got to Texas Tech that playing in the NBA was a reality for me, I wouldn't be harping on the effects of coaching in my journey and wouldn't be writing this book. It was a real dream and a real reality.

All I had to do was go to college and be a better version of myself. That happens with time, years, physical growth and opportunity. Time passed, years went by and I got physically stronger. But the opportunity, the opportunity was not there. Life and dreams are about provided opportunity. He was the end of my journey. Without the opportunity, he prohibited me from having a chance to be a college all American. He prohibited me from having a chance to be drafted into the NBA. He prohibited me a chance to be an NBA All-star. He prohibited me the chance to take care of my family like he took care of his. He prohibited me a chance to travel the world as I dreamed before I met him. He prohibited me a chance to make the NBA hall of fame as I had dreamt before I met him. It was my right and blessing to dream these things.

I worked very hard to put myself in a position to achieve these dreams. It was his responsibility, "COACH," to allow me the opportunity to achieve these dreams. Since he recruited me and somehow talked my dad into influencing me to come to Texas Tech, it was his responsibility to assist in my dreams. But he didn't. He did nothing. Not even a phone call or a good luck. He just moved on to the next group of players as Head Coach of Texas Tech University. Heartless. Simply heartless. Meanwhile for me, the struggles were just beginning. I was in a place I hadn't been since before I started playing Pee Wee baseball. I was nowhere. I was nothing. I was lost. I had nothing.

Not exactly, I did have something. Something I know a lot of families go through with a member of their family. I had a severe addiction. I was addicted to sports. I was addicted to winning. I was addicted to competition. I was addicted to dreaming. I was addicted to team. I was addicted to performing in front of crowds. I was addicted to practicing for something every day. I was addicted to stardom. I was addicted to basketball. Because it appeared basketball was over for me, my addictions were not being filled. Therefore, I did and still go through terrible withdrawal symptoms.

WITHDRAWALS

I didn't go to bed or wake up needing a drink. I never longed for the nicotine caused by cigarettes. Nor did I desire to smoke marijuana or long for a fix from heroin or cocaine. I went to bed and woke up needing basketball. I longed for the affect basketball had on my every day. I longed for the affect basketball had on my soul. I craved the way basketball made me feel. How basketball gave me chills. I desired and was addicted to an orange rock.

I never judged nor will I ever judge an alcoholic or any person addicted to any drug. I was more strung out on the high basketball provided than any person whose been addicted to drugs. I'd be out with friends or at a bar constantly checking the time. I'd be checking the time telling myself, "it's getting late Mason. You'd better get home so you can rest for practice tomorrow." Reality was, there was no practice the next day. There was no team. There was no basketball. But because I had had the same routine for 15 years straight, it was embedded in my mind, body and soul. Once the reality would hit me that there wasn't a practice or team to even practice with, I would start to feel pain all through my body. My body would feel constricted and tears would just flow down my face. People would be looking at me with a frightened worried look and would ask if I was ok. I couldn't explain to them what was going on. They wouldn't understand. They had no idea.

People who try to defend coaches' actions who treat athletes unfairly would say the education is the prize. They say athletes should be honored to go to college for free and get a degree. Reality is, it's not free. Athletes work their tails off daily and earn scholarships. They earn the right to dream. They bring in way more money to the university than the university gives them back. Whether the percentages are in the favor of the athlete to make it to professional sports or not, it's not the coaches right to prohibit or restrict the opportunity and the blessing. The education is not the prize. The education is earned through the love of sports. I went to class to pass so that I could play. I wanted to stay eligible because I wanted to continue playing.

When things were horrible during my Freshman and Sophomore season at Texas Tech, I didn't have the desire to go to class. Not going to class did not fix the basketball situation. I knew I was only hurting myself by not going. But when my love, passion and dream for basketball appeared to be fading away, so was my desire to achieve an education. The dream is the prize. The ability to achieve the dream is the prize. Without it, real personal and emotional problems will arise for athletes who desired but feel they didn't have the opportunity to fulfill it.

I'd played basketball every day I could since I was in the third grade. Even during football and baseball season, I played basketball every chance I got. I had terrible competition withdrawals. I felt like I was on an island alone with no help back to civilization. I'd wake up in the middle of the morning or from afternoon naps feeling I was late for practice or late for my game. My heart would be beating so fast and I would be very disoriented. Sometimes to a point where I had headaches and couldn't go back to sleep. I would be afraid to fall back asleep. Fearing the suffocating dreams which seemed so real, would reoccur.

Night after night, the dreams or should I say nightmares would occur. The worst would be dreaming I was playing in a game and I was free to be the Jerry "Bobo" Mason people loved to watch play basketball. It would feel so real. Right about the time I was going to do something spectacular, I would wake up. I would then realize that beautiful dream was just a terrible mirage. A terrible joke. A depressing moment in time. A nightmare. I would feel devastated but so exhausted because of the effort I was putting forth in my dream. I would be drenched in sweat. It was an embarrassing feeling. But there was no one there but me. Yet, I still felt embarrassed. I really thought or felt I was losing my mind. I didn't have a clue and felt I had no one to turn to. What I was losing was sleep. I would be so tired during the day. I would be so sad, lost and miserable. I was depressed and had withdrawals from many facets of my past.

Even though I felt I had no one to turn to or talk to, I knew God had a plan for me. I just couldn't imagine what it would be. I couldn't imagine him bringing me through so much pain and adversity to make this my reality. So instead of dreaming or having nightmares, I would cry, pray and talk with him. Here's my prayer:

PRAYER

AS THE TEARS FLOWED SOFTLY DOWN MY FACE, I CLOSED MY EYES TO

    PRAY,

THANKING GOD FOR MY PAST, AND HOPEFULLY ANOTHER

    DAY.

BUT AS I PRAYED, I BEGAN TO GET SELFISH AND LOSE MY TRAIN OF

    THOUGHT,

AND BEGAN TO EXPLAIN TO GOD THE TEARS AND WHY I FELT SO

    DISTRAUGHT.

"YOU SEE GOD, IM SO HURT AND CONFUSED AND I REALLY CAN'T

    UNDERSTAND,"

"WHY YOU ALLOWED HIM TO DO ME THIS WAY, WHY DID YOU MAKE HIM

    THE MAN?"

"YOU'RE THE ONLY GOD THERE IS, BUT YET HE HAD ALL THE

    POWER,"

"HE TOOK MY ALLY AND TURNED HER INTO MY ENEMY WHICH TURNED MY

SWEET DREAMS TO SOUR."

"YOU CAN'T DO THIS JERRY AND YOU CAN'T DO THAT JERRY" IS ALL I COULD

HERE HIM SAYING,

SO, I CLOSED MY EYES TIGHTER AND TIGHTER AS I CONTINUED CRYING AND

PRAYING.

"WHY GOD WHY, DOES IT HAVE TO BE ME, IN A POSITION SO

UNBEARABLE?"

I KNEW HE WASN'T GOING TO ANSWER ME AND THERE WAS NO ANSWER TO

THIS PARABLE.

AND IN THE MIDST OF CRYING AND PRAYING, I REGAINED MY TRAIN OF

THOUGHT,

KNOWING THAT I WAS ONLY FOOLING MYSELF AND IT WASN'T GOD'S

FAULT.

THAT THE CHOICE I MADE BECAUSE OF LOVE NOW HAUNTED ME ALL DAY

AND NIGHT,

I KNEW I HAD LOST MY LOVE IN THE BATTLE, BUT I JUST

COULDN'T LOSE MY

    FIGHT.

"PLEASE GOD, PLEASE HELP ME BREATHE. HE'S INVADED MY SOUL AND TAKEN

    MY OXYGEN AWAY,"

"PLEASE GOD I BEG OF YOU SIR, PLEASE DON'T LET HIM DO ME THIS

    WAY."

SO, I FINISHED THANKING FOR TODAY AND PRAYING FOR PEACE

    TOMORROW,

CRYING AND HOPING THE TEARS WOULD STOP FLOWING OR I JUST DROWN

    IN MY SORROW.

"THANK YOU, GOD. THANK YOU SO MUCH FOR BLESSING ME WITH THE

    OPPORTUNITY TO SHINE,"

"THANK YOU FOR ALLOWING ME TO HAVE A LOVE I CAN BE IN LOVE WITH,

    AS SHE IS SO DIVINE."

AMEN WAS THE LAST THING I SAID BEFORE I OPENED MY EYES TO THE

    DARK,

STILL FEELING THE PAIN DOWN DEEP IN MY SOUL BECAUSE

MY LOVE HAD

LEFT HER MARK.

JERRY

Night after night after night. Tears on top of tears on top of tears. Prayer after prayer after prayer. All because the passion and love I had for basketball. All because a man who was supposed to be a coach, ally and mentor didn't realize that basketball was my life. That my life without it wouldn't feel like life, but like survival. That his lack of compassion to not allow me the opportunity to fill my fix and feed my addiction would cause the rest of my life to be an internal rehabilitation center. No, I could never or would never judge another addict. No matter what they were addicted to. I had withdrawal symptoms that would have caused me to be admitted if I had seen a doctor.

Because of my addiction to that orange rock. Basketball was my life jacket in deep ocean waters. Basketball was my bible that provided my life, hope and the good word. Basketball was like a smooth ride in my dream car. My bullet proof vest that protected and shielded me during battle. Basketball was my eyes and light in the dark when I could not see. Basketball was the love I trusted and held tight at night. The medicine when I was sick that made me right. Basketball was in my head, my heart, my ears, my feet, my bones, my back and my fingers. Basketball was my body. Not only was basketball in my soul, basketball was my soul. So, without basketball, I was nothing and through the withdrawals, I felt every piece of pain of it.

I pray if you're a parent, you don't minimize the passion your kids can have in their soul for sports. I pray if you're a coach, you don't think you're the reason your athletes exist. That you don't presume you're the primary factor in your athletes' journey. I pray you know you are only an extension of the blessing. That you know it is your responsibility to give every athlete you coach the opportunity to achieve or fail trying to achieve their destiny. Coaches make sure that you aren't the reason why they fail. They will never forgive you. If you don't care if they fail or if they never forgive you, then you shouldn't be coaching.

The damage as a coach you can cause an athlete that works and desires but doesn't get a chance to fulfill those desires can be irreversible. Don't presume just because it's youth sports, Jr. High sports or High School sports withdrawals can't occur. Sometimes you and that sport is all an athlete has. Don't think because you have a degree and your life is good that your athletes' life will turn out the same way without your positive coaching and granted opportunity.

TRUTH WITHIN
THE NUMBERS

From my transition from dreamer, player into coaching I realize you can never teach who you never were. Coach Roberts couldn't teach me because he wasn't me. He wasn't me as a man or a player. Coach Myers couldn't teach me because he wasn't me. He wasn't me as a man or a coach. When I say they weren't me, I mean talent wise. I was a talent God made like no other. The difference is Coach Roberts understood that and was willing to help me, COACH me, in the areas I needed that he knew would enhance my talent. He knew by admitting my talent, appreciating my talent, enjoying my talent and helping me enhance it would allow me options and freedom.

But Coach Myers refused to let anyone's talent be bigger than his ego. He refused to let anyone's talent be better than who he was as player. He refused to let anyone's talent be bigger than Texas Tech. He was so selfish he didn't even realize he was prohibiting Texas Tech University from being a basketball power. A national contender every year. He didn't want to coach and assist. He wanted to control and humiliate.

Listen, I'm not writing this book to bash Coach Myers or make Coach Roberts a hero. I'm writing this book to tell my journey, truth and experiences with different coaches. All kids that play sports from youth until hopefully professional will experience different coaches. I consider my dad more detrimental to my journey than Coach Myers. So, I want to show how the factors are very crucial to the journey.

In my eyes, Coach Roberts was not a hero. I'm sure if you talk with him, he'd tell you he didn't want to be a hero. He was a coach who loved his job. He was a coach who appreciated his opportunity. He was a coach along with his family that loved us unconditionally. He was a coach that respected our tradition. He was a winner. He was a coach that allowed us to become winners and to continue the tradition. Within that, he allowed us to build our own identity and legacy. His legacy came from within our legacy. We all helped each other build our legacies. I will always, appreciate, respect and love him for that. Coach Myers on the other hand already felt he was a legend. He wanted us to bow down and respect his legacy as if we came to play college basketball to continue to build his legacy. From day one he made it clear that NO ONE would be a professional and NO ONE was bigger than his word and his beliefs. I told my dad that instantly. But he held strong in what he felt in his head. Which made me even more upset with him. It was like I was double teamed, and it was a trap between two powerful men who should have been the first two to set me free. Freedom is the key to the dream. Opportunity is the pathway to possible success.

Like I stated earlier on during my journey, I scored over 2,100 points, over 1,400 rebounds, over 200 blocked shots and over 250 assists in my High School career. All this in three seasons and without the three-point line. There was no three-point line in high school when I graduated in 1986. If so, I would have had over 5,000 points. However, I was able to attain these numbers because Coach Roberts trusted me and allowed me to be free and reach for the stars. By doing so, I became a star. I became an All American. I became a Division 1 athlete. While playing at Texas Tech I scored 886 points, I had 181 rebounds and 145 assists. I also had a few blocks, but nowhere near 200. 886 points with a three-point line. That's crazy. It's crazy because there wasn't or isn't a better shooter in the world than me. That's my opinion. However, if you're not going to let me shoot for the stars, at least let me rebound.

I got 1,800 rebounds worse in three years. Nah. Coach Myers wanted you to swing that ball for the best shot. I am the best shot coach. You knew that when you "recruited" me. But now, swing it? Then he stated he wanted the guards to get back on defense. "Don't rebound on the offensive end, get back and protect the basket." I had a 44, inch vertical jump. You knew that when you "recruited" me. But you don't want me to jump and rebound either coach? Wasted willing talent and ability. I would have done anything to play. Even allow you to make me look incompetent to the public. I know the competition level from High School changes and gets tougher. But my beliefs, skills and mentality didn't. No one on any level could prohibit me from being great and imposing my basketball beauty on them. No one except COACH.

For me, the big difference in the numbers came from opportunity and lack of opportunity. With the proper opportunity and trust from Coach Myers, I could have scored more points at Texas Tech University than I did at Lamesa High School. It was just a clash in vision, beliefs and desires. I blame that on my dad. He should have never interjected with his beliefs. But instead be appreciative of my work and blessing and let me trust my own want and gut.

Like I stated a few paragraphs ago, opportunity is the pathway to possible success. Here are more numbers to validate my beliefs:

Coach Myers was the head basketball coach at Texas Tech for 20 years. Coach Dickey, who proceeded Coach Myers as the head coach at Texas Tech was there for 10 years. In Coach Myers' 20 years, he has 6 of the top 20 scorers in Texas Tech History. Coach Dickey in his 10 years, has 7 of the top 20 scorers. Not that one is a better coach than the other, but the opportunities they allowed were very different. It's a matter of preference who one considers a better coach. I prefer the coach who loves his players enough to let them shine and provide a show for the fans who pay money to see a show. Contrary to what some coaches think, no one pays money to watch a coach, coach. Except maybe his family, if they even pay. More numbers:

While I played at Texas Tech, the top 6 players during that time attempted 3,338 field goals and 853 three-pointers. Notice I said top 6 players. The top 5 players who played for Coach Dickey attempted 6,472 field goals and 2,796 three-pointers. Notice I said 5 players.

It's all in the opportunity a coach is willing to provide. The players that played for Coach Dickey were excellent players. I know them all. But if Coach Myers would have allowed us to take 3,134 more field goes and 1,943 more three-pointers I guarantee the tops scorers would be different. I guarantee the team I played on with all the talent, our outcomes would be much different. We were all winners and came from winning programs and tradition. But collaboratively, we were modified and programmed into basic basketball players. No room to breathe, no room to grow, no room to shine, no room to create, no room to win. Therefore, there was no room for us to succeed an attain opportunities and dreams outside of Texas Tech. Not one player I played with played in the NBA. But we all dreamt too. Several of us had more than enough ability to play in the NBA. But it's hard for teams to take a chance on you when your numbers don't add up and your reference and COACH doesn't vouch for you or the numbers, he allowed you to attain. However, because Coach Dickey allowed his players to build a legacy for themselves via Texas Tech, he had 6 players play in the NBA. They all know me. They all know my talent and ability. They all know I was NBA talent before any of them were. But they came at the right time with the right COACH. Coaches and opportunity parents. Coaches and opportunity.

I feel very fortunate and blessed to have been able to work to be an elite athlete and college basketball player. I don't want the accomplishments or failures of my journey to dictate the emphasis on the importance of being with the right coach at any level. If I had experienced bad coaches during youth sports, during Jr. High or High School I may not have had a chance to accomplish all I did during those journeys and become a Division 1 athlete. Each level has its' own importance.

The hope and prayer is that an athlete never experiences one bad coach during his or her journey. However, it happens more times than it doesn't. Parents do your homework before joining any team or attending any school. It wasn't Coach Myers' fault I attended Texas Tech. I had done my homework and knew he was a bad fit for me. But, all the factors (peers, parents, coaches and yourself) must be aligned for possible success to occur. The factors aligning are important on each level and summer sports as well. Withdrawals and depression can occur at any time during and or because of sports. Not just in college or the beginning or end of an athletes' journey.

EMPTINESS AFTER
THE JOURNEY

How can a young man become a man when he'll never be complete? How can a man be a complete spouse if he's not complete? How can a man be a great and complete father if he's not complete? How can a man long for love when loving hurts? These are some of the things I've had to fight to overcome in my mind and emptiness. I know to some and maybe many this seems absurd. But for me it was and is real. The withdrawals and effects from the withdrawals are real. The pain is real and it's everlasting. When you wake up every day for a common goal and that goal no longer exist, it leaves you empty. Especially when you want to fulfill that goal because it has so many levels and people attached to it.

When your mind, heart, soul, the well being of your family and your existence depends on that goal, it gets fragile without it. It hurts more when the outcome of the goal desired to be fulfilled is affected by someone else. If I had gone to Seton Hall University and attained the same results, I would have accepted my responsibility and have moved on 30 years ago. It's all about having the chance to be in control of my own destiny. Being able to be accountable for my work or lack of work. Being able to create my own opportunities within the opportunity. It's easier to take accountability for failure that way.

However, no parent or coach should interfere or refuse a kid from getting a chance to try and complete his path. A chance to fulfill the passion, dream, emptiness and the habit. I wasn't the best friend because of the emptiness. I wasn't the best father because of the emptiness. My relationships, both business and personal have suffered because of the emptiness. The journey with Coach Myers hurt me deep. It not only affected me, if affected generations. It affected my relationship with my dad and my sons. I was unable to be the best son for my dad after the journey with Coach Myers. I love my sons tremendously and they know that. But internally, because I was so ruined, I wasn't the complete dad for them I needed to be.

Repairing and making amends for my lack of presence has been a journey of its own. More than anything, I feel sorry for Coach Myers. I feel sorry for him and every coach that's afraid to be secondary in their players journey. I feel sorry for him and every coach that interject and control their players journey instead of trusting growing with their players. I feel sorry for him and every coach that goes home at night with his feelings being more important than those of their players. I feel sorry for him and every coach that are content and fulfilled in their journey and blessing but leave their players empty.

It wasn't until I became a coach that I was able to start healing. It was an opportunity for me to help as many kids and athletes pursue their dreams and journey. Coaching gave me the opportunity to let kids know that they are the prize. So many coaches think the world revolves around them. They are so stubborn and refuse to change for the betterment of their players. I say stubborn, but selfish would be a better description. So many coaches are quick to blame their players when things are going wrong. But when things are going good, they take the credit for being a great coach. A coach is nothing without his players but an individual collecting a check. I assume Coach Myers was making good money. He never shared that. He also didn't discuss with us how we can make the same money he made or more.

Selfish. Since I've been coaching, I've used the box of crackerjacks in my analogy. I tell the kids, "you are the prize in the crackerjack box and there's only one prize. The coaches are the actual crackerjacks and peanuts in the box. There are plenty of them. "So, don't let an entire box of crackerjacks and peanuts make you feel you are not the prize." It is an amazing blessing to be a coach. To be able to gain trust from kids and their parents that you will do your best so that they may achieve their best.

While being the head basketball coach at Ennis High School, I was blessed to coach my son Jordan. He didn't start his basketball journey as early as I did. In fact, it wasn't until his 7th grade year in Jr. High that he decided he wanted to be good at basketball. Ironically, my 7th grade year in Jr. High is when I thought my basketball journey had come to an end because of my broken foot. But his journey was just beginning. It was very tough as a father and coach not to be too hard and overbearing on him during his journey. I discussed earlier about parents coaching their kids and not being so tough on them that they want to quit. I've been there.

Coaching Jordan (22) was a challenge and a blessing. But it was also a challenge and blessing to coach each one of these young men. We were and still are family. This group won district and 26 games this season. 7 of these young men continued their journey after Ennis playing college sports. 5 played college basketball and 2 college football. A coach can be beneficial in all sports journeys. Not just one sport.

However, there may not have been a better blessing God bestowed upon me to be able to coach my son. In fact, there may not having been a bigger blessing God bestowed upon me than to be a Coach. In my ten years of being a head basketball coach, I've been blessed to assist eight young men in earning college basketball scholarships. Including my son Jordan. Even more importantly, I've been blessed to coach hundreds of athletes who didn't receive basketball scholarships. However, because of the opportunity to play basketball and have the freedom to chase the dream, they found their own path to success. They learned how to work hard every day. They learned how to work hard every day knowing the result of the hard work would benefit them. Not benefit me as a coach. They learned how to accept love, respect and discipline. They learned how to show love, respect and discipline themselves. They learned how to win and become winners. They learned how to be an integral part of a team. They learned how to be primary within the team. They learned how to be accountable for how they won, lost and what they received from both.

Even though they didn't earn a college basketball scholarship, they earned valuable life lessons that allowed them to be successful in society. They were able to build their own identity and legacy. To me, that's what being a coach is all about. Being able to assist the ones who have the ability and blessing to continue their journey to the next level. But also, allowing all your players to chase the same dream despite their ability or DNA. Allowing all your players the freedom to attain if they work hard every day and do things the right way.

Coaching is a selfless profession. It's a profession where coaches think less of themselves and their schemes and more of their players and their dreams. I'd advise parents and coaches to assist in the journey and allow what God has in store for them to dictate the rest of their destiny. However, the assistance from parents and coaches is very crucial to the present and future of the journey for their kids. I will never heal from my journey completely. I feel that. However, coaching has been great medicine and great motivation in my healing process.

As a coach I won district championships and playoff games in Ennis and Terrell. Me being a winner and loving winning, I loved the trophies we received. However, it's nothing compared to fun, challenges, passion, friendships, relationships and immense love I have and built coaching all my players.

FAMILY FIRST

Family first. This is one of the core values that was instilled into my family and many other families I was around. My brothers, sister and I heard it all the time from our parents. "No matter what happens, always put your family first. No matter what." Family first. In most families nationwide, sports are intertwined in their culture. Whether it's baseball, basketball, football, wrestling, soccer, hockey or whatever sport, kids and families are participating in sports. Sports are a major component that bonds families and break families apart. We are all committed as parents to making sure our kids are happy. That means if our kids love participating in sports, we as parents are participating in those sports. If our kids are happy, we are happy.

Sports allow our kids to be relevant and allow our kids to feel. Sports allow our kids to grow and more importantly, sports allow our kids to dream. Because of sports, families are recognized by their last name. Even in youth sports, kids are tied to a parent by their last name and the popularity of that parent from sports years ago. Even though my brothers, sister and I were descent in youth sports and progressing our way up, we were tied to my dad because of his achievements in sports back in the 1960s. In most places in Texas, when people here the last name "MASON," they instantly tie the last name to Lamesa and basketball. It's where we are from and who we are. Sports define us. Not just the "MASONS," sports define us all.

So, which is more important? The family or the happiness of your kids? Such an unfair question I know. However, this is when or where sports bond families together or break them apart. This is when certified but nonqualified coaches have the upper hand on the capable and qualified coaches. This is when the importance of providing for your family coincides with the importance of providing happiness for your kids. This is when the four factors clash and the elements within each pull at the core value, Family First, and put it to the test.

Even though I was the head coach, I was also a parent. Because Ennis was such a tremendous football powerhouse, I had to decide as a dad was it the best town for me and him to build basketball tradition with half or more of the basketball players playing football. As parents, you must make the best decisions for your kids and your family.

FAMILY DECISIONS
VS. THE "RULE"

I know you thought I was being sincere and intimate when I was discussing the importance of "Family First." I was. But, now for the purpose of the understanding, I'm about to pit the importance of the family against the importance of our kids love for sports. This is not a conflict that occurs originally within the family. It's a conflict that occurs because of the rules that are put into effect to govern sports that families are required to abide by. I want to make sure when I stated earlier in the journey, "make sure as parents you do everything possible for your kids to have a chance," that as parents, you are doing everything possible.

The state of Texas has the UIL governing its sports. UIL stands for University Interscholastic League. The UIL produces and regulates the rules for all sports in Texas that are under the UIL umbrella. One of the rules and forms that is required to be filled out by schools and parents once a family moves is the "Previous Athletic Participation" rule and form. This when a family moves from one state to another, district to another or school to another. For an athlete to be eligible to play sports at another school or in another district, this form is required to be filled out by the previous and current school. Administrators and coaches from each school are required to sign off on the form and the form must be approved by the governing board for an athlete to be eligible to participate.

The parents or legal guardian of the athlete must sign off on the form as well. If any portion within this PAP form is not approved, then there's a possibility the athlete won't be eligible. It mainly prohibits an athlete from playing varsity sports if not approved. The rule is a very effective tool to prevent cheating in UIL high school sports. A section to be filled out on the PAP form is the "Parent Residential Rule." This form within the PAP form is very powerful. It is in place to eliminate the possibility of cheating in Texas and their high school sports.

I've been in high school coaching for 23 years and seen how this rule has enhanced stability in sports. But I've also seen this rule affect the journey of many athletes. Not because the rule isn't needed or fair, but because of some tough decisions parents and families are required to make because of what rule states. The rule is put in place to make sure that a parent, parents or legal guardians of the athlete reside in the district that the athlete participates in.

Here are some of the questions asked under the "Parent Residential Rule":

1. "Does the student live with one parent, both parents, guardian, foster parents?"
2. "Are the parents of the student married, never married, married-living apart, divorced, deceased?"
3. "Does the parent(s) of the student reside outside the attendance zone of the school the student wishes to represent?"
4. "Is there a change in schools but no change in address?"
5. "Is there more than one residence owned, rented or maintained by the parents?"
6. "Are any members of the family still residing at the previous residence?"
7. "Are there other family members in grades K-12 at-

tending a different school district other than the school district the student is now attending?"

Very personal and precise questions. How the parent(s) answer these questions dictate where they go from there with that question. Also, the answers to these questions must be validated by the previous school and verified by the school the athlete is trying to attend. I believe they are all valid questions and are required to help prevent cheating. But from these questions I want to establish accountability not only for the athletes and parents but for all involved in the process.

By the time some athletes get into high school, living residency has already been established by their families. Established sometimes because a parent or both parents work in the area or parents like a school or district for academic reasons. Rarely do parents choose a school or districts because of sports concerns or needs for their kids.

When they do, their intentions are questioned and reviewed through the PAP process. This is where conflict and life changing decisions are made or not made.

I've tried to establish throughout my journey the importance of parents finding the appropriate school, situation and coach to enhance the possibility of achieving the dream. But what if a family has already bought a home and established residency in a district when a new coach is hired? This family has a kid that has college scholarship potential, but the new coach hired doesn't have the coaching ability or experience to help athletes on that level. Because of the Parent Resident Rule, that family and athlete must stay at that high school even though they know their child isn't getting what he needs on his path to achieving an athletic scholarship.

This happens a lot in high school sports. Families bound to a school or district and mediocrity because of their residency. Athletes being cheated of the coaching and opportunities they need to pursue their happiness and dreams. Because of the rule, the responsibility falls on the parents or guardians to burden the pain and frustrations of their kids if they aren't happy and fulfilled. But no accountability falls on the administration for hiring incapable coaches to fulfill the destiny of their coaches.

If the family doesn't sell their home or leave the district but sends their kid to another school for the fulfillment, the kid loses his eligibility and year. So, which is more important, the house or the happiness of the kids? It's a tough situation to be for parents. Sometimes coaches won't sign off on the athletes PAP form even if the family moves. They may make the argument the family moved for athletic purposes which is illegal under the PAP guidelines. But there's nothing under those guidelines that hold the coach accountable.

As a player, parent and a coach myself, I know athletes and parents don't leave a good thing and a blessed opportunity. I know the PAP is put in place to protect the integrity of high school sports. But what is in place to protect the dreams and aspirations of high school athletes?

AAU, SELECT AND CLUB SPORTS

AAU, Select and Club sports have become very beneficial and crucial in the assisting of providing opportunities for athletes to continue their scholarship dream. When I was coming through youth sports and high school, none of these opportunities existed. We had all stars for basketball and baseball, but there weren't any college coaches nor recruiting going on. As I stated earlier during my high school journey, I attended one national BCI summer basketball tournament in Phoenix Arizona. That was my only AAU type exposure to college coaches. So, the chances of been seen nationally in the 1980s were very slim.

Today, there's AAU for basketball, Select for baseball and Club teams for volleyball and soccer. The good thing about fall, summer and spring leagues or teams is that they start during youth ages. Kids are almost able to participate in the favorite sport or sports all year long. The bad thing is that these leagues or teams can become very expensive. But year after year, parents are searching for that extra assistance to help their kids fulfill their athletic passions and dreams.

Unless kids are with a sponsored organization, the fees sometimes become unbearable. Fees consist of monthly fees, uniform fees, practice or gym fees, tournament fees, meal fees and travel fees if the clubs travel. All those fees with no guarantee that their child may not earn or receive an athletic scholarship at the end of the journey. Also knowing, that If they don't travel to the sanctioned tournaments, their likelihood of being seen by college coaches decline. Sanctioned tournaments are tournaments that are approved by the NCAA for college coaches to be in attendance. Because of these tournaments, kids are being seen and some recruited as early as Jr. High school.

Here is where a lot of problems begin because of AAU, Club and Select sports. Because kids are now being seen and some recruited earlier, parents are under more pressure to make sure their kids are participating. If not, they feel their kids are and will be left behind. So, they continue to pay so that their kids can play. I know personally that there are AAU basketball organizations that start as early as the 3rd grade. So, you have some kids doing that for 9 or 10 summers straight hoping for an opportunity to receive an athletic scholarship. It's kind of like the saying, "keeping up with the Jonses'." No matter the financial burden on the family, the pressure to be a part of the madness, keeps families coming back. If a family has multiple kids playing the same sport or a different sport, the financial burden becomes that much more stressful on the family.

Again, I stress, there are not guarantees at the end of the journey that a scholarship will be received. The kicker is, if the kids do it the possibility remains. If not, it is virtually impossible to receive an athletic scholarship. That's because of NCAA recruiting guidelines. During high school sports seasons, college coaches can only be out on the road watching kids during certain periods of time during the year. When they are out, they are attending games watching the elite players who have made a name for themselves during their club or select season. So, for a lot of small school athletes or athletes that don't play club sports, they are rarely seen or recruited.

As a parent with kids that love sports, there is no way around it. Either you accept the financial stress or deprive your kids of opportunities that MAY assist in their journey. Even though I was a high school head coach, I had to make the same decisions for my son. I could have counted on the great basketball seasons he had at Ennis High School for him to be recruited. However, I saw for myself the lack of college coaches attending the games and tournaments we played in. So, for him to get the exposure he needed, I had to accept the financial burden and get him on a traveling AAU team. No one is immune to the expenses these club, select and aau fees required for kids to be a part of their organization.

As a parent and coach, I am proponent of AAU basketball. But I am a firm believer that if the high school coach and AAU organization is not on the same page for the betterment of the athlete, the athletes' chances for a scholarship goes down. 7 of these 9 athletes received college basketball scholarships and had good college careers. 1 went on to be drafted and play and in the NBA. It wasn't all because of AAU, but AAU played a major role in their opportunities. 4 of them played for me at Ennis High School and the others had great coaches at their respective high schools. Coach Pat coached this team and made sure to collaborate with each head coach. It's imperative.

THE CON,

THE CLASH, THE END

The only guarantees with club, aau and select sports is that the tournament directors and owners of the organizations are making tons of money. No matter what age group or nationally sanctioned tournament the teams travel to, there's no guarantee that college coaches will be there or see them if they are there. There is a guarantee that most if not all of them will leave there without a scholarship offer. However, the fees must be paid. That's the con of the all these organizations and tournaments. They don't guarantee parents that if they have their kids for years in their organization that they will receive a college scholarship. The tournament directors don't guarantee that each team will be on a field or court where college coaches are viewing. The only thing guaranteed is parents will have paid tons on money for a hope.

Being a high school coach and hosting some aau tournaments, I've had the opportunity to hear from a lot of high school coaches and be around a lot of aau owners. The clash and most disturbing conclusion I heard and witnessed is most high school basketball coaches hate aau basketball and aau basketball organizations think they are more important that high school basketball coaches. Therefore, because of both of their feelings and thoughts, the only losers in the situation is the athletes themselves.

Once athletes enter 9th grade, the aau, select and club owners should be joining with the high school coaches in their sport to provide a continuous plan for athletes to get better all year.

Both should be on the same page for the betterment of the athletes instead of trying to be primary in a journey that doesn't belong to them. Reality is a number of these organizations don't have enough qualified coaches to even be coaching during the journey. So, if a kid has a journey with a nonqualified high school coach and incapable aau, select and club coaches, the journey ends.

Parents, don't not pay attention to the expectations required for high school coaches because you think they have aau, select and club sports to fall back on. Make sure to hold both accountable to work together for the betterment of your kids. It defeats the purpose to have a great high school coach and a horrible coach for your club team and vice versa. Especially for the time and money you'll spend during these club sports and the restrictions families are under with the Residency Rule.

Also, parents be careful searching for ELITE teams and sponsored teams. Not that they aren't great, but the needs of the athletes because of the ELITE or sponsored can be neglected. When I say ELITE, I'm encompassing sponsored teams as well. They are great because all those fees parents paid when they weren't sponsored go away. The uniforms, shoes, tournament fees, hotel and travel fees are all paid by whomever the team is sponsored by. Another pro with ELITE and sponsored teams is that they probably have many highly ranked kids and kids receiving college recruitment attention.

So, being a part of one of these teams assures visibility to colleges and college coaches. However, the more ELITE players on one team, the harder it is for the needs of each kid to get the individual help he needs on his deficiencies. Most of these teams get these ELITE kids from all over the city or state for specifically for a skill they are good at. So, when they join the team, they are expected to do just that. However, to be able to play more on the next level, they will have to do more than what they did in high school. Some of these ELITE and sponsored teams keeps athletes one dimensional. But when they go to college, they will be required to do more than just that one perfected skill. Make sure that if your kid joins ELITE that he is getting the ELITE work from an ELITE coach that he needs.

ACCOUNTABILITY

I am putting a lot of emphasis on the rule, but the emphasis should be put on the reality. The reality is there are tons of schools where coaches are incompatible, insufficient, have no compassion and not knowledgeable enough to fulfill the needs and dreams of their athletes. So, what do the parents and athletes do? I knew and it was confirmed after the first day with Coach Myers that Texas Tech and Coach Myers wasn't a good fit for me. Like a lot of parents in tough situations, my dad didn't listen to or better yet digest what I was telling him.

Also, the coaches will paint a picture of what the athlete is not doing or needs to do. Then they will say if the athletes do these things, the opportunities will get better. Parents that grew up earning their way will be empathetic to the promises made by coaches. Because they have those values, they will want their kids to earn what they desire. However, in feeling that way, parents sometimes give coaches a scapegoat for being accountable for helping their kids. There is a difference from a kid being pushed to be hard working and persistent than a coach depriving a kid from a chance to dream and chase those dreams. Some coaches make it all about them and their ability to control the narrative.

Coach Myers had the authority and it was his way or no way. However, the picture he painted for my dad and the public was that I was the problem. It's easier for both to believe a kid can be the problem because most assume because he's a coach, he can't be wrong. As a coach, I believe in holding athletes accountable. But holding them accountable for working to achieve what they themselves desire to achieve. Not holding them accountable for what I need them to achieve for me. As a coach, I also believe there should some accountability taken for coaches who only try to get what's best for them from their athletes. But have no desire or intention to help their athletes attain the maximum of their abilities, work ethic and dreams.

I'm going to shift the emphasis from the reality to the administration. I feel the administrations of the school districts should be responsible for holding coaches accountable for the needs and desires of the athletes. They are the ones who interview and hires the faculty and staff. Being hired as a teacher/coach myself, I know the process before the hiring. Some of the process includes reference checks, a background check, fingerprinting and certification verification. All are necessary to protect the districts from liability and surrounding students with criminals and the wrong people. It is an extensive but very important process. Another step along with the checks is making sure the teacher/coach is certified in the field and sport required. Once all the boxes are checked, if desired, the employee is hired. Throughout the hiring process, the administration is trying to hire the proper personnel to teach their students and help them learn and grow.

Once a teacher/coach is hired, they have met all the qualifications needed. But, are they really qualified to fulfill minds, hearts, souls and dreams? Or are they only qualified to be hired. Remember earlier in my journey I talked about the difference between certified and qualified. Teachers/coaches must be certified to be hired. Administrations and parents can only pray that they are qualified. It's easy to find out if they are certified. It's documented. However, the qualified trait in a teacher/coach shows in the results of their students and athletes. So, what if the results of the teacher/coach don't fulfill the expectations of the administration, parents and students. Who's held accountable for that teacher/coach?

Not all coaches have college level athletes in their program.

However, it's their responsibility to teach, work and push their athletes as though they are college level athletes. It's not their right to utilize the athletes' deficiencies or lack of ability to control the narrative and not allow them to dream. That starts with youth sports coaches and works its way through each level of coaches. Coaches must be qualified enough to understand the level of athletes they have. If they have athletes that have college potential, it's their responsibility to enhance that talent so that the athletes do receive an athletic scholarship. When coaches do have talented athletes and the athletes feel they are being deprived or cheated, that's when a lot of residency problems begin.

It's not always the coaches. Some athletes may feel or think they are better than what they are. However, a qualified coach would know the level of each athlete and communicate that with each athlete and their parents at the beginning of their journey. It doesn't matter what level is. Then as a unit, they will start building toward the aspirations of the athlete and not stay stagnate because of the thoughts of the coach. But when coaches do have high level athletes and don't fulfill the potential of those athletes, who holds those coaches accountable?

The administration should hold them accountable because they are the ones that hired the coach. Accountability doesn't mean firing on the spot in my eyes. It means getting an understanding from the coaches, parents and athletes. Then making the best decision for all parties concerned. However, if the decision of the administration is to side with the coach, that coach shouldn't have the power to prevent the family and athlete from moving on by not signing off on the PAP form.

No athlete or family should be allowed to dictate a coaches' employment. However, no coach should be allowed to dictate an athletes' journey. The results of the athletes will dictate how qualified the coach is. It is the coaches responsibly to make sure his players produce within the taught system but with freedom to showcase their abilities. If not, it's the administrations responsibility to get a coach in there for the athletes who can. If the administration refuses to do that, the family and athlete should be allowed to move without the people who failed them having a voice in their next journey.

THE PEG LIST

Districts are paid money for every kid in their district. That's why attendance of the students is so important to the districts. Attendance is also important so that the kids can learn, grow, graduate and hopefully go out into society and be productive citizens. However, it's not the money that makes those things possible for the students. It's the teachers that are hired responsibility to teach and advance the kids. But teachers are paid from that money so therefore expectations are placed on those teachers.

If academic expectations are not met, accountability falls on the teachers. From there, accountability falls on the school then the district. If after a probationary period the district continues below expectation academic state results, that district is placed on the PEG List. The Public Education Grant List. The PEG List is part of the Texas Education Code. The PEG List basically says that if a campus is a low performing campus on this PEG List that a student or students can attend another district. It also says that the district the students attend must have open enrollment before they can attend that district. When a campus in on this PEG List, it also allows students to attend another campus without living in the district of the campus they attend.

In my eyes, it's an outstanding rule because it demands AC-CONTABILITY. Yes, academics are very important and so is sports. One may be more important than the next. It just depends on who's assessing the importance of the two. However, they both should carry the same weight when it comes to accountability.

Just like the PEG List, there should be a rule to govern the accountability of coaches. Sports require just as much and important teaching as the classroom. If coaches aren't reaching expectations and getting the desired results for the athletes, the athletes should be allowed to attend another campus without living in the new campus they attend.

I'm not saying this to upset or discredit coaches and coaching. I'm a coach and I hold myself accountable to the same expectations. I do see it as an opportunity and a blessing for us coaches to be great for God's greatest gift to us, our kids.

So, I ask again, which comes first the family or the rules? Really, neither should come first. What should come first is the passions, desires, needs and dreams of the kids. But for good measure and fairness, the rules are set in place and must be obeyed. I see the Residency Rule as a rule to restrict and prohibit. But I see the PEG List rule as a rule that demands and protects. That's just my opinion. But knowing that the rules are in place, families should do their homework about the sports and coaches of a school before they allow their kids to attend. If a family is already in school district when a coaching change is made and it doesn't benefit their journey, the family should be prepared to make life changing decisions or work with the administration of the school to make a decision that's best for all the athletes not just one.

My advice to parents is to find a place for your kids that has a coach that will love them unconditionally. A coach that will not only assist in the journey but will also enjoy the journey of your kids. A coach that when your kids journey ends with the coach a new journey begins for the both. Find a coach who will love your kids forever and who your kids will love back. A coach who is willing and grateful to be a reference and friend through all journeys of life after the athlete leaves the coaches program. A coach who will be family for life and who is always there, no matter what.

Unfortunately, I didn't and don't have that relationship with Coach Meyers. Since I finished playing basketball for him at Texas Tech in 1990, I can count on my fingers the conversations him and I have had from 1990-2020. He was my mediator during the most important and crucial journey of my life. But today, there is nothing. He's never done anything for me or helped me in any way since I left him in 1990. I know he didn't love me while I played for him. I don't think he knew how to love. If he did, I never felt it. Really, I don't think he knew me at all when I played for him. I was too advanced and complex in my beliefs for him to take the time to know me. He didn't want to know me, who I was and how I got to be who I was. He had his mind made up from day one when I got to Texas Tech, he didn't care to know me because he knew he was going to try and change me.

This story sums up everything I have always known and felt about Coach Myers. In 2019, my brother from another mother, James Gray, was getting inducted into the Southwest Conference Hall of Fame. He was a star running back at Texas Tech University while I was attending playing basketball. I was there to support him and be a part of his beautiful honor for his accomplishments during his journey. As I was standing in the hallway about to go be seated, I saw Coach Myers walk right by me. An attendant was telling me which tables were for the Texas Tech alumni. Coach Myers walked up as she was talking. After she walked off, here's how the conversation went. He asked me, "are you here with Texas Tech? If so, those three tables at the back are for Tech alumni." I just looked at him. The kid in me was hurt because I knew he didn't know who I was. As I was looking at him and him looking at me, I asked, "you don't even know who I am do you?" He responded in a whispering voice, "no I don't believe I do." Then he asked me the funniest, most humiliating and most hurtful question, "did you used to block for James Gray?"

Thirty-four years since he convinced my dad to convince me to go against one of the biggest decisions of my life. Thirty years since I played for him. Four years of pain, struggle, neglect, heartache and depression behind this man and he asked if I was a blocker for a running back. Thirty years later, he's still the most selfish, inconsiderate man I've ever known. I didn't know whether to laugh or curse him. I responded in an angry voice, "I have never blocked for anyone sir. I slaved for you for four years." I said, "I'm Jerry Mason." He was stunned. He touched me as if I was a ghost. He blamed not knowing me on my suit, hat, facial hair and of course not weighing what I weighed in 1986. It was a very uncomfortable moment for the both of us. Me running into the man that ruined everything for me. Him running into the kid he knew he'd ruined. I didn't expect him to know me thirty years later when he didn't even know me when he coached me.

Coach Roberts on the other hand has always been there for me, my brothers and my family. Him and his wife Kathy have invited us to his family events. They have been to my home, our home and our family events. Coach Roberts has been a reference for my brothers and I and been very instrumental in all of us being head coaches. He's supported our programs in person and from afar. Not only for me and my family, but Coach Roberts is still a part of all my teammates and his other players lives. He was not only an awesome coach, but an awesome friend. Still to this very day. He's forever earned the title "COACH" from me.

During my high school journey, Coach Roberts stood behind me and allowed me to build a legacy for myself. Today, he stands beside me as a friend. That's what makes him a great coach. L to R: Dwight Hines, me, Cedric Mason, Chris Mason and Wayne Roberts. Mr. Hines is the newspaper man who told me after my Sophomore year journey I couldn't shoot. After I proved him wrong, we became family as well. We are at my mom and dads' 50th year anniversary.

FANTASY TO REALITY

SWING BATTER BATTER, SWING BATTER BATTER, SWING BATTER BATTER, SWING,

FREE AS A SPIRIT LOVING BASEBALL AND THAT'S WHEN I KNEW SPORTS WAS THE THING.

THE BEAUTIFUL COLORS OF THE UNIFORMS AND THE DIFFERENT SOUNDS FROM ALL THE BATS,

ALL THE DIFFERENT CHARACTERS AND THEIR BASE-BALL RITUALS AND THE DIFFERENT VERSIONS OF CREASED UP HATS.

FOOTBALL, BASKETBALL AND BASEBALL IS WHO WE WERE. THESE SPORTS WERE US AND OUR LIFE,

UNTIL THE CRACKING SOUND FROM MY RIGHT FOOT THAT HURT LIKE THE STABBING FROM A KNIFE.

COLD AND ALONE I SAT BESIDE THE CREEK WITH MY FOOT SNAPPED INTO TO,

CRYING WITH TEARS FROZEN TO MY CHEEKS AND MY FOOT THROBBING WITH PAIN, I DIDN'T KNOW WHAT TO DO.

I COULD JUMP SO HIGH JUST YESTERDAY BUT NOW I COULD BARELY WALK,

THEN A CAR DROVE BY AND I WANTED TO SCREAM, BUT MY VOICE WAS FROZEN AND I COULDN'T YELL NOR

TALK.

"I'M GOING TO DIE OUT HERE TONIGHT," I SAID TO MY-SELF, "BUT IF I DON'T THIS WILL BE MY STORY."

"THAT I WILL TELL AND USE TO HELP OTHERS IN THE DESPAIR AND TO GOD WILL BE THE GLORY."

I COULDN'T TELL IF THE FEAR I WAS FEELING WAS OF DYING OR NOT BEING ABLE TO PLAY SPORTS ANYMORE,

BUT WHICHEVER ONE IT WAS SENT A NEEDLE THROUGH MY BODY AND STUCK ME DEEP IN MY CORE.

I THANK GOD I DIDN'T DIE THAT NIGHT, BUT IT WAS THE FIRST OF THE WORST TWO YEARS OF MY LIFE,

THE PAIN, THE HEARTACHE, THE LONELINESS, THE FEAR, THE DEPRESSION LED TO MY INNER STRIFE.

FOR TWO YEARS I FOUGHT A BATTLE WITH MYSELF SAYING I CAN'T THEN, SAYING I CAN,

BUT ONE DAY MY LUCK CHANGED AND I GOT A BLESS-ING FROM A GOOD MAN.

FROM THERE THINGS BEGAN TO SMOOTH OUT AND IN BASKETBALL I BEGAN TO EXCEL,

I COPED WITH MY FRIENDS, GIRLS AND SUCCESS OH SO VERY WELL.

AND I FELT DEEP WITHIN MYSELF I WAS ACHIEVING ALL I POSSIBLY COULD,

BUT I KNEW THAT SOONER OR LATER GOOD TIMES

WOULD END AND INDEED THEY REALLY WOULD.

FOR WITHIN THE NEXT FEW YEARS, ALL THE FRIENDS I USED TO HAVE I BEGAN TO LOSE,

I DIDN'T SPEND AS MUCH TIME AS USUAL WITH THEM BECAUSE I WANTED TO PAY MY DUES.

TO BE THE BEST SCHOOLBOY AND HOOPSTER AROUND AND ADVANCE TO A HIGHER LEVEL,

BUT MY FRIENDS AND I DIDN'T SEE EYE TO EYE, SO THEY DISPOSED OF ME LIKE DIRT FROM A SHOVEL.

NONETHELESS, I CONTINUED TO WORK HARDER AND HARDER AND FROM THAT I BEGAN TO GET BETTER,

HOPING FROM ANY COLLEGE BASKETBALL PROGRAM, I WOULD RECEIVE A LETTER.

ACKNOWLEDGING ME FOR ATHLETIC ABILITY AND ALL THE HOOPS I MADE,

ALSO RECOGNIZING THROUGH ALL THE TOUGH TIMES, I COULD MAKE THE GRADES.

THERE WERE NO LIMITS TO WHAT I COULD DO, AS EVIDENT BY THE NUMEROUS AWARDS I RECEIVED,

BUT THERE WAS SOMETHING THAT HURT ME DEEP, WHICH WAS MY FRIENDS WHO NEVER BELIEVED.

THAT WHAT I WAS DOING WAS NOT TO SHOW OFF, BUT INSTEAD MAKE MY LIFE COMPLETE,

TO BE ABLE IN MY PRESENT AND FUTURE TO FACE ANY

OBSTACLE AND ALWAYS BE WILLING TO COMPETE.

SO, FROM THERE I FELT I HAD TO DO WHAT I HAD TO DO AND CONQUER MY DREAMS ON MY OWN,

BECAUSE IF I WAITED FOR THEM TO FINALLY REALIZE THAT, MY DREAMS WOULD PROBABLY BE GONE.

THANKFULLY I CROSSED THE CHALLENGES OF HIGH SCHOOL WITH MY TALENT AND MY KNOWLEDGE,

NOW I WAS OFF TO VISIT A NEW TOWN WITH MANY NEW CHALLENGES, THE PLACE WE ALL CALL COLLEGE.

MY DAD HAD INTERJECTED HIS BELIEFS IN MY JOURNEY, SO I WENT TO A COLLEGE HE THOUGHT I COULD MASTER,

BUT I KNEW IN MY HEAD AND FELT IN MY HEART THAT HIS DECISION WOULD PROBABLY END UP A DISASTER.

IT WAS SCARY IN THE BEGINNING, BUT I ADJUSTED TO THAT, BECAUSE I KNEW I WASN'T ALONE,

ALTHOUGH FROM MY FAMILY, HOUSE AND SO- CALLED FRIENDS, I WAS REALLY GONE.

I KNEW ON THE CAMPUS THERE WERE KIDS LIKE ME WHO FELT THEY COULD NOT COPE,

WITH THE FASTER LIFE AND ALL THE PRESSURES AND WANTED TO HANG THEMSELVES FROM A ROPE.

BUT I'M STILL HERE AS YOU CAN SEE, I DID NO SUCH THING AS HANGING,

EVEN THOUGH I FELT THAT UNTIL I GOT ACCUSTOMED, MY HEAD WOULD NEVER STOP BANGING.

FINALLY, THE PRESSURE OF BELONGING GOT BETTER, AND EVERYTHING SEEMED TO FALL,

INTO PLACE, LIKE I'D HOPED FROM THE START, EVERYTHING EXCEPT BASKETBALL.

BECAUSE OF ALL THE WORK I HAD PUT INTO MY CRAFT, THIS HAD ALWAYS BEEN EASIER TO COME BY,

BUT COACH HAD MADE BASKETBALL MY ENEMY AND I FELT IF IT DIDN'T GET BETTER, I WOULD RATHER DIE.

I FELT AS IF I WAS NEW TO THE GAME AND THROUGH HIS EYES I HAD TO RELEARN,

BECAUSE COMING FROM BEING A STAR TO NOTHING, I GUESS HE FELT I HAD TO WAIT MY TURN.

"DON'T SHOOT THOSE SHOTS, THIS ISN'T HIGH SCHOOL BALL," IS ALL HE'D EVER SAY,

"YOU CAN'T DO THIS AND YOU CAN'T DO THAT," IS HIS WORDS SO THAT I WOULD NOT PLAY.

ALL YEAR LONG ALTHOUGH MY GRADES WERE GOOD, I BEGAN TO GET MORE AND MORE DOWN ON THE GAME,

BECAUSE FOR THE PEOPLE WHO EXPECTED GREAT THINGS FROM ME, I WAS VERY ASHAMED.

TO FACE THE FACT THAT HE WASN'T ALLOWING ME TO BE THE OUTSTANDING PLAYER I HAD ONCE BEEN,

THE JERRY "BOBO" MASON WHO LED HIS TEAM TO NUMEROUS VICTORIES AND THEY KNEW WOULD ALWAYS WIN.

BUT LIKE THE TRUE COMPETITOR I AM, I FACED ADVERSITY AND I PRAYED IT WOULD SOON STOP,

FOR ONE DAY IN KNEW IN MY COLLEGIATE CAREER, I WOULD EVENTUALLY BE ON TOP.

OF THE WORLD, OF MY DREAMS AND EVERYTHING I'VE ALWAYS WANTED.

BUT HE WAS SUCH A SELFISH COACH AND WITH HIS DISCOURAGING WORDS MY DREAMS HE ALWAYS TAUNTED.

AS THE NEXT YEARS PASSED SOME THINGS GOT BETTER, BUT A LOT WERE RUSTY,

BECAUSE WHILE IN HIGH SCHOOL I COULD SEE MY FUTURE, IN COLLEGE MY VISION WAS DUSTY.

MY CONFIDENCE WAS LOW, MY GRADES BEGAN TO PLUMMET, BUT THE GIRLS WERE REALLY FLOWING

AND I BEGAN TO GET CAUGHT UP IN THE MIX AND IGNORING BASKETBALL AND PRETENDING NOT KNOWING.

NOW EVERYTHING WAS IN REVERSE AND I WAS REALLY LOST,

BECAUSE I FELT HE HAD TURNED ME AGAINST MY LOVE FOR BASKETBALL AND I KNEW IT WAS GOING TO COST.

ME THE HAPPIEST TIMES OF MY LIFE AND MY DREAMS OF BECOMING A PRO,

BUT HOW TO DEFEAT THIS MAN AND OVERCOME HIS NEGATIVITY I TRULY DID NOT KNOW.

AS IT CLOSER AND CLOSER TO THE END, I COULD SEE IT WAS GOING TO BE A TRUE DISASTER,

BECAUSE I KNEW WHAT I HAD SET MY GOALS AND DREAMS ON, I WOULDN'T BE ABLE TO MASTER.

"WHERE WAS MY HEART AND COMPETITIVENESS I HAD ONCE ACQUIRED,"

"WHERE WAS THE JERRY MASON THAT SO MANY PEOPLE HAD ONCE ADMIRED."

WAS IT MY SOUL SPEAKING TO ME, TELLING ME I HAD MADE A BIG MISTAKE?

OR WAS IT MY FEELINGS, EMOTIONS OR CONSCIENCE TALKING TO ME, TELLING ME MY DREAMS WERE FAKE?

I COULDN'T TELL YOU BECAUSE I DIDN'T KNOW, BUT I DID KNOW WHAT I WANTED SO BAD,

WHICH WAS TO DO WHAT WAS RIGHT, ACCOMPLISH GREAT DEEDS AND REACH THE STATUS I HAD ONCE HAD.

IT WASN'T IMPOSSIBLE I FELT TO MYSELF BECAUSE I HAD DONE IT ONCE BEFORE,

AND IF I COULD DO IT RIGHT BACK THEN, WHY NOT DO IT RIGHT ONCE MORE?

SO, I TRIED AND SUCCEEDED AS PLANNED AND DE-CIDED TO LET NATURE DO THE REST,

BECAUSE I FELT AS FAR AS FIGHTING ADVERSITY, JERRY MASON HAD DONE HIS BEST.

AND TODAY I'M HERE BECAUSE I NEVER GAVE UP, AL-THOUGH MY DREAMS ARE ALL BATTERED,

I ALSO REALIZE THROUGH MY UP AND DOWNS, THAT BASKETBALL IS NOT ALL THAT MATTERED.

FOR THE LIFE I LIVED UNTIL THAT DAY COULD WELL BE CALLED A FANTASY,

WHEREAS, THE LIFE I LIVE FOR THE REST OF MY LIFE, WILL ALWAYS BE MY REALITY.

DREAMER

Made in the USA
Monee, IL
14 July 2020